"I met Julie almost 10 years ago. When I started my company in early 2022, I knew immediately to reach out to her for help setting my marketing direction. The first thing she did was help me learn how to think about my LinkedIn® page and how to make the most of it, as well as how to be an intentional poster of content. In this book, she shares the same practical, yet genius, advice with her readers, enabling them to maximize the value they can get from the service. In a world full of relentless over-sharers, I particularly appreciate how her book articulates various "buckets of content" that should be shared, along with the internal and external value from each one of those."

Rebeca Snelling
Author of *Choosing By Advantages* and
Leadership Coach at RS Consulting

"Bringing your B2B business onto LinkedIn® can be a challenge, but it can also offer huge rewards. With this book, Julie is breaking down the barriers to demystify how this tool can become one of the most valuable assets for business growth and success. With real examples and tangible advice drawn from her years of guiding companies and leaders through this process, Julie is the perfect guide for anyone who is ready to make a real impact, now."

Catlin O'Shaughnessy Coffrin
Founder & CEO, Captivating Consulting, LLC

"Having witnessed Julie's skills in action for many years, I can attest that she is one of the best at meeting professional business development goals. Before reading this book, I didn't realize how increasingly important LinkedIn® has become for personal and company branding. The best part is that Julie breaks it all down in a manner that kept my interest to continue learning more about this valuable tool and how I can meet my own professional goals."

Vickki Villegas
Interior Design Studio Director,
studiotrope Design Collective, Denver, CO

"Julie Wanzer is the 'go-to' for digital marketing in the construction and engineering industries. In her book, you will find that her passion for both, as well as her expertise, leaps off the pages, but you don't have to be in construction or engineering to benefit. Her tips and guidance can be applied to any industry that needs to have a strong digital presence, and if you are doing business today, you need a strong digital presence. As you read through her book, you will feel like one of her clients. It's as if she is taking you by the hand and walking you through the process. Her four characteristics of a meaningful post and specific examples of how to do it were so helpful, and I just loved her end of chapter tips broken down by Novice, Intermediate, and Experienced. I will definitely refer back to this book again and again."

Donna Marino, PsyD
Psychologist/Executive Coach

"Like it or not, your presence on LinkedIn® is no longer an optional nicety in today's professional world. What you choose to share develops a brand that current and future clients, colleagues, and employers will use when making critical decisions about their interactions with you. Wanzer has developed a comprehensive guide for you to create a strategic online image that truly represents what you want others to know about you as an individual or an organization. While working with the author for more than five years, I have experienced firsthand how she uses methods described in this book to successfully shape a brand by making the right choices about original content, reposts, and timing. After reading the book, you will have a step-by-step process to help you discern these important choices for your own brand."

Heidi M. Gordon, CAE
Executive Director for the American Council
of Engineering Companies of Colorado

"Marketing design and professional services can be a challenge because the audience you need to reach is often niche and can be entangled in personal relationships. LinkedIn® provides a platform that allows you to target these specific networks, but it's critical that the tone and content of your posts align with your personal and professional branding. In this book, Julie provides both a conceptual framework and specific advice on how to achieve this balance."

Tom Otteson, AIA
Project Manager, Shopworks Architecture

"I used to think LinkedIn® was just 'Facebook for businesses.' I jumped on board with my former and current company profiles and very little about myself. After having met Julie, I was enlightened with greater understanding of what a powerful connection tool LinkedIn® really is. Her knowledge, experience, and hands-on discovery in the early days are invaluable. Thanks to Julie, I'm now refreshing my profile and am learning better ways to utilize LinkedIn® for a more enhanced business development and networking experience."

Tim Ernest, PE, SE
Project Development Manager, BKBM Engineers

"There is a certain amount of hesitancy I have always had when it comes to creating and maintaining multiple social media accounts in today's world. They can become difficult systems to properly manage, and many professionals struggle to commit the correct amount of time and resources towards them. The many ways these systems can be utilized by an individual to their personal advantage and their company's betterment is apparent in so many ways, but many of us need help to be effective and efficient. If there are credentials that validate expertise within the realm of forging a commanding online presence, Julie Wanzer should not only have them as a designation, but she should also be consulted as a resource to define the metrics to obtain them. Her knowledge in this space is complemented by her ability to help her clients learn ways to tell their stories in a unique and compelling manner. I would heed Julie's opinion and guidance regarding many things, and the content of her first book is most definitely one of them. Enjoy!"

Moses Alvarez
Director of Training, Colorado Contractors Association

"Julie and I met at an SMPS Southwest Regional Conference. I listened to her presentation on leveraging your personal brand on LinkedIn® to build trust, illustrate thought leadership, and generate leads. I was immediately drawn to her energetic and welcoming personality, as well as her insightful perspective.

The most valuable takeaway from the book is that it breaks down the process of creating an effective personal LinkedIn® brand into two manageable and actionable steps. Julie provides well-thought-out examples, detailed strategies, and concrete calls to action throughout her book. I highly recommend this book to any individual or organization looking to strategically build its presence on the social media platform. Indeed, Julie's book is a must have for anyone looking to 'up their LinkedIn® game.'"

Jessica Ray
Vice President of Business Development,
Naranjo Civil Constructors, Inc.

"Julie Wanzer knows the truth about business. Namely that people want to do business with those that they know, they like, and they trust. In Get Them To Care, Julie unpacks those all important 'two millimeter changes'—the things you cannot afford to miss out on if you want to develop a highly effective online presence. One that will help you and your company to attract and win the right business and unlock the power of relationship building at scale. Whether you are just getting started or are at advanced stages of building your online brand and business, Julie's practical tips will get you on a fast path to better visibility and customer conversion."

Sam Lee
Founder, IndeCollective

GET THEM TO CARE

GET THEM TO CARE

How to Leverage LinkedIn® to Build Your Online Presence and Become a Trusted Brand

Julie Wanzer LEED AP

PYP
Academy
Press

For permission requests, write to the below address:

PYP Academy Press
141 Weston Street, #155
Hartford, CT, 06141

PYP
Academy
Press

The opinions expressed by the Author are not necessarily those held by PYP Academy Press.

Ordering Information: Quantity sales and special discounts are available on quantity purchases by corporations, associations, and others. For details, contact the author at julie@increasingmarketvalue.com.

Edited by: Kassandra White
Cover design by: Julia Kuris
Typeset by: Medlar Publishing Solutions Pvt Ltd., India

Printed in the United States of America.

ISBN: 979-8-88797-051-6 (hardcover)
ISBN: 979-8-88797-050-9 (paperback)
ISBN: 979-8-88797-052-3 (ebook)

Library of Congress Control Number: 2023906897

First edition, September 2023.

Publish Your Purpose is a hybrid publisher of non-fiction books. Our authors are thought leaders, experts in their fields, and visionaries paving the way to social change—from food security to anti-racism. We give underrepresented voices power and a stage to share their stories, speak their truth, and impact their communities. Do you have a book idea you would like us to consider publishing? Please visit PublishYourPurpose.com for more information.

CONTENTS

PART I

PERSONAL LinkedIn® BRANDING

COMPANY LinkedIn® BRANDING

ACKNOWLEDGMENTS

I wrote my first book. I feel even more accomplished seeing it in print, and I have finally checked off something from my to-do list, which has been there since I was 13 years old. At that age, I begged my parents to enroll me in a writing coach class that involved one-on-one instructions and assignments via snail mail, where I would wait with bated breath staring at the mailbox for my next assignment to arrive in an over-stuffed envelope. Thank you to my mom and dad, Carol and Chris Wanzer, who obliged me so many years ago and who have supported me ever since. My mom is a talented writer and has encouraged me since I learned to write to keep a journal, to write often, and to challenge myself through the written word.

I also need to thank my grandfather, Charles Clark Russell, who ended up paying for my initial writing class. I only found this out recently, when exchanging stories about him at his funeral in September 2021 in Stillwater, Oklahoma, when he passed at the age of 100. He was also known for his love of writing, and I still have a few of the handwritten letters he sent to me over the years.

I want to thank my fiancé, Blake Stine, for bearing with me through my bouts of writer's block and always greeting me with a freshly cooked gourmet meal to keep me writing. And for being an incredible source of love, support, and gratitude for the life we are building together.

I would also like to thank Sam Lee, founder of IndeCollective, for introducing me to Jenn T. Grace at Publish Your Purpose, who made this book a reality for me. I enrolled in IndeCollective in the fall of 2021 not knowing how many doors it would open for me, with this one being the most rewarding thus far. Jenn and her team, especially Bailly Morse, have been a true source of guidance, support, and even therapy for me during the most difficult moments of completing this manuscript. I could not have asked for a better partner in this book publishing process. I would also like to thank Marlene Kurban for writing a strategic book description, Kassandra White for editing this book, and Julia Kuris for designing the book cover.

Had you told me eight years ago that I could build a business around social media, specifically on LinkedIn,® I would have told you that you are absolutely batshit crazy.

Yes, I curse. I work in construction. And this is my story.

In September 2015, I decided to rip off the proverbial corporate chains I found myself in and ventured out on my own to start Business Rewritten, Inc.—a marketing communications firm for the architecture/engineering/construction (A/E/C) and commercial real estate industries. I have been building my connections on LinkedIn® since 2011, both with industry associations and via the business development I was initially providing for an engineering firm and later, an architecture firm.

I was consistently connecting with people on LinkedIn.® Every time I went to an industry event or a construction site tour or even a municipal pre-proposal bid meeting, I judiciously collected people's business cards and instinctively sent each person a LinkedIn® request to help me learn people's names, faces, and interests.

By the time I officially opened Business Rewritten, I had over 500 connections on LinkedIn® that I strategically mined, to reach out to and book coffee meetings, lunches, happy hours, and industry networking events. I also reached out to former colleagues, asking for recommendations on LinkedIn® and endorsements of my various marketing and communications skills on LinkedIn.® I then started posting construction data reports and insightful articles about marketing for the design and construction industry.

Currently, I have over 1,600 connections (I recommend quality of connections over quantity, see Part I, Chapter 4) and manage 10 company LinkedIn® pages. I also provide LinkedIn® profile review services, where I lead executives through an assessment of their current profile and interview them about their goals—both personal and professional—to help them tell their compelling story on LinkedIn.®

Without knowing it at the time, I was subconsciously creating and building my personal online brand and leveraging it to build my business. Social media marketing and online business development is now 80% of my revenue—where I live, breathe, and eat. It helps me learn the LinkedIn® language and allows me to share the tips and tricks I have honed over the years with you, the reader.

Managing both your personal and company's online presence and branding is no longer an option but an obligation in today's digital world. Critical decisions are being made about you and your company, by both your potential clients and employees, as to whether they want to work with you and your firm, based on your personal LinkedIn® profile and your company's profile.

This book allows you to learn more about how to tell a compelling story online that highlights your personal expertise and your firm's differentiators to win more work and recruit and retain top talent.

Get Them to Care: How to Leverage LinkedIn® to Build Your Online Digital Presence & Become a Trusted Brand is split into two parts:

- Part I: Personal LinkedIn® Branding
- Part II: Company LinkedIn® Branding

It also contains a variety of best practices to guide you, whether you identify as a LinkedIn® novice, a LinkedIn® expert, or some variation in between.

Interspersed throughout the book, you will find the following to help you improve both your personal and company profiles:

- LinkedIn® Profile Examples
- Calls to Action to make updates on LinkedIn® (Get on LinkedIn®)
- Frequently Asked Questions (FAQ's)

This book is meant to be a trusted resource for you and a reference guide on how to build and manage both your personal and company-wide brand online. Feel free to flip back and forth between Part I and Part II, scour the book for all of those Calls to Action on LinkedIn® designed for you and your company to win more work, or judiciously read this book from cover to cover.

No matter how you read it, here's what you can expect to glean from this book.

Part I Takeaways:
- Enhance your personal digital profile
- Become a trusted resource for your professional network
- Make strategic digital connections to win more work and build business opportunities

Part II Takeaways:
- Improve your company's digital presence
- Rebuild your company culture to focus on retainment and recruitment
- Establish your firm's expertise in the marketplace

ASSESSMENT: LET'S TAKE A POLL

First, let's take a poll and find out where you land on the LinkedIn® spectrum. This will also help identify the lens under which you view and read this book.

1. **How often are you on LinkedIn?®**
    a.   *My LinkedIn® is tied to an old business email that I can't access anymore*
    b.   *Once a month*
    c.   *Once a week*
    d.   *Every day*
    e.   *Multiple times a day*

2. **What are you currently using LinkedIn® for?**
    a.   *To find a new job*
    b.   *To find out where people I know are working*
    c.   *To make strategic connections*
    d.   *To post on my company's LinkedIn® page*
    e.   *To manage both my personal and company LinkedIn® profiles*

3. **What is currently on your LinkedIn® profile?**
   a. *An old(er) headshot and the last company I worked for*
   b. *Current headshot, current company name and title, and my current job description*
   c. *All of b., plus an introductory paragraph in the "About" section, and associations I participate in*
   d. *All of c., plus "Skills" and "Recommendations" sections endorsed by others*
   e. *All of d., plus a personalized tagline, personally branded "About" section, and "Volunteer" and "Interests" sections completed*

4. **How are you managing your company's LinkedIn® profile?**
   a. *I didn't know my company had a LinkedIn® page*
   b. *I know my company has a LinkedIn® page*
   c. *I follow my company's LinkedIn® page and click "Like" on some of the posts*
   d. *I am regularly sharing my company's LinkedIn® posts and sending content to our Marketing team to post on LinkedIn®*
   e. *I manage my company's LinkedIn® page and set quarterly strategies and goals based on LinkedIn® "Analytics"*

If you answered mostly A's and B's = Novice LinkedIn® Level
If you answered mostly C's = Intermediate LinkedIn® Level
If you answered mostly D's and E's = Experienced LinkedIn® Level

Use this assessment to help you complete Calls To Action based on your particular level. Each chapter includes a "Get On LinkedIn®" section immediately following it that relates to the subject matter of that chapter.

There is also an online *Resources* page that accompanies this book where the reader can reference images and links to information mentioned throughout the book by scanning the QR code, like this one.

Call To Action

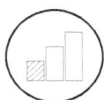

Novice = Add your middle initial to your profile to help identify "catfishing." This will help you identify when you receive a connection from a bot. It will say something like "Julie M.—I would like to offer you a job in accounting" instead of a message from an actual person that would most likely start with "Julie—Let me know if you're looking for a job, we have some opportunities for you."

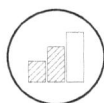

Intermediate = Add your professional designations (LEED AP, PE, PhD, MBA, etc.) right after your last name on your profile, so they automatically show up wherever your name is listed. This establishes your credibility upfront and helps build trust that you are an industry professional. It also saves people time from having to find your professional designations hidden in your profile. You worked hard for that MBA, and everyone should immediately see and recognize that.

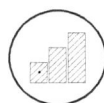

Experienced = Add a section to your profile for "Providing Services" [NOTE: Do this whether you are a consultant or full-time employee] and create your own personalized services page that supplements your personal profile. On your personal profile page, click on "Open To," then select "Providing Services," and then create a services page that includes a short intro bio, the skills/services you are best at, and media files (images) for examples. This helps to establish and build your personal brand on LinkedIn® by highlighting what you like to do and providing a visual representation of your career through the media files and examples you provide.

Get on LinkedIn®

I always love an impactful "Before and After" post, where you can track your progress and demonstrate that you are making strides to improve.

BEFORE: Before reading any further, take out your cell phone, pull up LinkedIn,® and take a screenshot of your current LinkedIn® profile.

AFTER: After completing this book, take another screenshot of your profile wherever you've made the biggest changes.

Then, post on LinkedIn® and tag me (@Julie M. Wanzer, LEED AP) with the hashtag #LinkedInBeforeAfter.

Lastly, scan the QR code to view one of my #LinkedInBeforeAfter moments that I recently made.

PART

PERSONAL
LinkedIn®
BRANDING

INVEST IN YOURSELF: ONLINE PERSONAL BRANDING

1

> TALKS ABOUT:
> #PersonalBranding #DigitalBusinessCard #OnlineBrand

If you have ever flown on a commercial airline, there is always a sequence of safety announcements presented by the flight attendants as the plane is taxiing towards the runway. One part of these announcements always stuck in my mind and, quite honestly, took me a long time to grasp. In the event of an emergency, oxygen masks will be released from overhead, and, as always:

"Be sure to secure your own mask before assisting others."

Simple enough, but as a born and raised "people pleaser," I always felt that helping others first was more important. Almost 40 years later, I have finally wrapped my head around the notion that you HAVE to take care of yourself first, or you will have nothing left to give others.

While the flight safety reference may seem a bit outlandish when it comes to protecting your online personal brand, the idiom still rings true in this instance, in that, before you can be a trusted resource and connector for others, you have to invest in yourself first to create and protect your personal online brand.

I would even go so far as to state that managing your personal online presence is no longer an option, but an obligation, in today's digital world. Critical decisions are being made about you by both your potential clients and company employees, as to whether they want to work with you and your firm, simply based off of the information they can source about you online.

I understand that based on the generational diversity in the current workplace—with Gen Z'ers just entering the workforce, Millennials hitting their mid-career milestones, and Baby Boomers who can't or just don't want to retire yet—this notion of online personal branding is still fairly new and did not exist in the 1990s/pre-internet age. If you were quoted in a local trade publication, like the *Colorado Real Estate Journal,* or lucky enough to be featured in a national publication, like the *New York Times,* you had to purchase the publication, scour through every page until you found your name, make copies of the article on the Xerox® machine at work, and perhaps even purchase additional copies to frame or keep in your personal portfolio. Then, the story would be archived in a filing room somewhere in the basement, only to be resurrected by interested parties who were familiar with the library filing system and could manage scrolling through tons of microfiche to maybe stumble upon the article where you are mentioned.

Today, someone does not even have to leave the comfort of their own bed to find out personal information about you. They can source every article you have ever been quoted in, all in a matter of milliseconds. According to Oberlo's article entitled, "10 Google Search Statistics You Need to Know in 2022":[1]

> *"The latest data shows that Google processes over 99,000 searches every single second (Internet Live Stats, 2022). This makes more than 8.5 billion searches a day (Internet Live Stats, 2022)."*

The moral of the story is that people can easily find out anything they want about you online in a matter of seconds, whether you like it or not, so you might as well tell your own story and control the narrative.

To find out how your current online personal brand is performing, I encourage you to simply Google your first and last name and current city where you reside to view the search results. Typically, your LinkedIn® account or other social media platforms will appear within the first few search results, which is what most people will click on first. According to the Advanced Web Ranking's January 2022 Report,[2] 50 percent of the total click-throughs go to the first three listings for non-branded search queries. Translation: If people are searching for you online and your LinkedIn® profile is what appears in the first three search results, then be sure to tell a compelling story about yourself online.

Why LinkedIn®?

Based on your assessment from the introductory section, your range of knowledge and experience with LinkedIn® may vary,

---

[1] Source: Oberlo, "10 Google Search Statistics You Need to Know in 2022" January 2, 2022. https://www.oberlo.com/blog/google-search-statistics#:~:text=We%20know%20that%20there%20are,Internet%20Live%20Stats%2C%202022.

[2] Source: https://www.advancedwebranking.com/ctrstudy/. Also https://www.smartinsights.com/search-engine-marketing/search-engine-statistics/.

from not really knowing what LinkedIn® is and how business professionals are using it to understanding why LinkedIn® has become one of the most effective social media platforms for the new B2B (business to business) lead generation.[3] Let's review some of the most recent statistics to understand the basic premise of LinkedIn® personal branding.

As of March 2022, there are 810 million LinkedIn® users, as reported by Microsoft's Quarterly Earnings report. [NOTE: Microsoft owns LinkedIn®]. With 185 million users in the U.S. alone, there is clearly a movement on LinkedIn® that you need to be a part of to manage your personal online brand.

Among all 810 million users, what are they using LinkedIn® for? According to LinkedIn's® 2021 report, "Why B2B Marketers Build on LinkedIn,®" 63 million people attended virtual events on LinkedIn® in 2020, and there are 2.9 million industry-related groups on LinkedIn® that professionals can join and engage with.

Overwhelmingly, people are using LinkedIn® to share content. In fact, 96 percent of B2B Marketers use LinkedIn® to distribute their content, according to the 2021 report. This helps support the case that LinkedIn® is considered the most effective social media platform for B2B lead generation.

The design and construction industry is a service industry where we are constantly communicating with and competing against other B2B service providers. When you are evenly matched with another person or firm on cost and schedule, the only other differentiating factor is quality. One way to make yourself stand apart from others is to drive home that you are a quality individual who consistently helps others and shares relevant resources. Use your personal platform on LinkedIn® to generate worthwhile content and share it out with your connections.

---

[3] Source: LinkedIn®, Return to Growth 2021 Report "Why B2B Marketers Build on LinkedIn®".

By sharing relevant and timely information via your personal profile, you begin to establish yourself as a trusted resource. In my experience, the biggest connection point that people are missing on LinkedIn® is being a RESOURCE! In order to set yourself apart from others and manage your personal online brand, you need to build relationships with people online and engage with them. How do you start these mutually beneficial relationships? The simplest answer is by helping others. So, if you are sharing resources or industry news, plus tips and tricks that others may not have seen before, you have now opened that door and taken that first step towards a mutually beneficial business relationship.

Get Them to Care About You

In this digital age where we are constantly connected and have access to streaming news and information 24/7, telling your story and getting people to care about you has become that much more challenging. One way to share your story and differentiate yourself amongst your peers is to personally brand yourself online via your LinkedIn® personal profile.

Personal LinkedIn® Profile: Why do I need one?

When I am hired to consult with design and construction firms about their professional online branding on LinkedIn,® one of the very first objections I receive is, "Why do I need a profile? Everyone in the industry already knows who I am."

My favorite story to tell in response to that question is: A few years ago, in 2018, I was hired by a design firm to implement a company-wide LinkedIn® strategy for not only the firm itself on LinkedIn,® but also for their leadership team. And of course, one of the principals asked me on the first day I arrived, when we were all seated in this big conference room, "Why do I need a profile, Julie? Everyone knows who I am." I replied, "Well, sir, you do have a great reputation, and you are very well known, but how are you representing yourself online?" He said, "I'm not even on LinkedIn.® I don't need to be." I probed further and asked, "Aren't you the PIC (Principal in Charge) when interviewing for firm-wide projects to win work?" And he said, "Oh, of course, I'm always there." I then relayed to him the following story:

When I first started my company in 2015, I was producing a lot of proposals, and within that realm, I was invited to be on a selection committee. The owner flew in from Texas and was running late for the interview selection process, where we had a whole day of interviews planned out. While the first team began setting up for their presentation, people from the prospective project team and the selection committee team were exchanging business cards. One participant, the owner of the project, was not really engaged and just sat on his phone. He was taking notes during the presentations, but still looking down at his phone the entire time. We breezed through the first morning, and during our break for lunch, I couldn't help but ask the owner, "Hey, so, are you really paying attention during these interviews? I couldn't help but notice you've been on your phone the entire time. We're all here to help support you during these interviews. This is your project, after all." And he responded back, "Oh, no, I'm just doing my research," and I asked, "What?" He leaned over to show me his notes, and he had written: "No LI" or "LI Wrong." I followed up with, "What is LI? In our architecture/engineering/construction (A/E/C) industry there are tons of acronyms, and I thought I knew almost all of them." He looked me dead in the eye and said "LinkedIn,®" and I sat there wide-eyed and almost embarrassed, responding with just an "Oh."

He went on to say that "No LI" was written for each person that showed up for the interview but didn't have a LinkedIn® profile, and that was an automatic "ding"/negative indicator for that person. The next bit of scribble that read "LI Wrong" indicated that he had looked up that particular person on LinkedIn,® and the person's profile had listed the wrong company or at least not the company that the person was supposed to be representing at this interview. After further investigation, it turned out that the interviewing principal had just changed jobs, was at the interview with his new firm, but had never updated his LinkedIn® profile to show that he had started at this new company. His LinkedIn® profile actually showed that he was employed by a competing firm.

I found it very interesting that this owner continued in this manner throughout the whole day of interviews. He did not know anyone from the interviewing teams, was not familiar with the Denver design and construction industry and did not have a pulse on the quality of the various A/E/C service providers at the interview. This owner was making his impressions, or rather *receiving* his first impressions of people, simply from searching their personal profiles on LinkedIn.® So, if you walk away from this book having learned nothing, please make sure all of the principals at your firm have a LinkedIn® profile, and, at the very least, make sure it lists their current firm and has a current picture.

Digital Business Card

One of the best ways to shape your personal online brand is to treat your personal LinkedIn® profile as your digital business card. Some of us can recall actually maintaining a physical Rolodex® of business cards on our desks or storing a huge stack of business cards at the bottom of our cabinet filing drawer—but who has the time to digitally input all of those business cards, so you have easy access to them when you're not at your desk?

The day before my February 2021 presentation, "LinkedIn® Business Development & Marketing Best Practices for the A/E/C Industry" for the American Council of Engineering Companies of Colorado (ACEC Colorado), Dana Mansell, the Associate Director at ACEC Colorado, relayed this story to me as we were reviewing my presentation together the day before the event.

She told me that she was already in the habit of collecting these digital business cards. She explained that after attending a conference or an event, she would take all of the business cards she had collected, go home, send each of those people an invitation to connect on LinkedIn,® then throw that person's business card away. This is a great business development tip: Use LinkedIn® as a follow-up mechanism with people you have just met (whether on a Zoom® call or at an in-person event). By reaching out and connecting with them via LinkedIn,® you can grow your professional network and search for more connection points with those people. Perhaps you learn that someone you just connected with attended the same university as you or shares similar volunteer interests. Typically, that information is not included on people's printed business cards, but it is readily available on their LinkedIn® profiles.

Another way to think about it is to consider your LinkedIn® profile as the "cheapest" but most convenient business card you will ever have. There are no printing costs, and LinkedIn® is free to join. It is a platform that keeps all of your professional connections and information about them in one place that you can easily access on the go, without carrying around that awkwardly shaped Rolodex®.

In this same vein, your LinkedIn® personal profile also acts as your personal online resume. There are so many different options and portions of your profile where you can really build out your career portfolio. Again, if someone is just taking a quick glance at your LinkedIn® profile, they can readily see that you have done a project at UC Health or that you have a strong interest in local volunteer opportunities or that you are in the middle of attending business school.

All of these things say a lot about you, and you haven't even opened your mouth yet to speak with this person. Without saying a word, people can find ways to make a connection with you based on your personal profile, begin to learn more about your personal brand, and understand more about how you are a trusted resource for others. Invest in yourself now and take control of the digital narrative being told about you online in order to build mutually beneficial business development relationships.

At the end of each chapter, you will find a Call to Action exercise based on the poll you took at the beginning of the book, designating yourself as a Novice, Intermediate, or Experienced LinkedIn® user. This "choose your own adventure" style book allows you to progress from Novice to Experienced or choose all of the combinations in between.

Get on LinkedIn,® Section 1

Once you're ready to invest in yourself and take control of your personal online brand, you can sign onto LinkedIn® and implement one—or all—of the below tactics.

Novice = Make sure you are an active and engaged participant on LinkedIn® by bookmarking *linkedin.com* on your desktop or laptop browser, downloading the LinkedIn® app on your smart phone, and saving your login information.

Check your personal profile photo to make sure it is a current (within the last two years) photo of just yourself that serves as a professional headshot. If I am meeting with someone I have never met with before, I often check that person's LinkedIn® profile photo before we meet, so I can spot that person at my local coffee shop for our introductory meeting.

Make sure your current job title and company are accurately reflected on your personal profile. This simple action helps create trust in you among your connections and those looking you up on LinkedIn,® showing them that you are proud to share where you are currently working.

Intermediate = Update your profile to contain relevant information about your career path beyond just a company name and previous job title. I typically recommend including at the minimum, your very first job and relevant roles along your career trajectory where you made a significant impact. You do not need to list every single job you have had since you were 18 years old or positions where you only stayed a few months.

Instead, include important career milestones and/or achievements from your work history that help tell the story about where you started and how you have grown in your career. Listing past companies and your impact at those firms helps others create connection points with you. For instance, someone grazing your profile might learn that you both worked at the same company, but at different times, or that you were previously employed by a competitor and that you could contribute insights that could benefit that new company.

Experienced = Go beyond your day to day work history to include a more complete story of your personal brand. Be sure to include all of the organizations and associations that you are a member of and how you choose to spend your time outside of work—perhaps serving as a board member or volunteering at your local community center to teach underprivileged children how to read.

Including information beyond just your typical "nine-to-five" job experience helps you break ground on your personal profile and begin to establish your personal brand about who you are, what you care about, and how you choose to spend your time. At the end of the day, people like working with people they like, so the more you can reveal about yourself, the more connection points people have to get to know you better and find out what it's like to interact with you.

BREAK GROUND ON YOUR PERSONAL PROFILE

2

TALKS ABOUT:
#PersonalProfile #PersonalBranding #TellingYourStory

Although I have been an active participant on LinkedIn® since 2011 and have professionally managed over 25 different LinkedIn® personal and business profiles, I myself was hesitant to embrace the fact that I needed my own personal brand. My first instinct was to reject this notion by telling myself that only celebrities, politicians, and influencers need a personal online brand. But, once you embrace the fact that people can search online to find out almost anything they want about you and form their own opinions based on the information they find, it's up to *you* to control the narrative and tell an impactful and intentional story about yourself.

Where to Start

In order to create your narrative online and build your personal brand, let's first dissect the various parts and pieces of your personal LinkedIn® profile to ensure you are telling the whole story. LinkedIn® has certainly changed over the years as the platform has evolved, but these are the latest best practices you can take advantage of on your personal profile.

Let's start at the top section of your profile—or rather at the "top of the fold" as we say in "print media speak"—that loosely creates your first impression, or the first bits of information that others can learn about you. This initial section typically contains your headshot, background horizontal photo, full name, tagline, location, and top interests.

First and foremost, make sure that little circle at the very top of your profile contains a current headshot. I reiterate that, back in 2018 when I was hired by that design firm to implement some LinkedIn® strategies, one of the principals I was consulting for did have a profile, but the profile photo was noticeably from 20 years ago. Overall, the photo had a yellowish hue and a dark backdrop, but what dated his photo the most was all of the dark hair covering his head. I glanced back up from his LinkedIn® profile to compare the digital visual to the physical visual sitting across from me. Both claimed to represent this gentleman, but I couldn't help but notice the absence of hair and how light in color it was, with the addition of reading glasses permanently affixed to his face.

I understand that over the course of your career, you will inherently favor one professional headshot over another, but when you attend networking events, present at project interviews, or participate in online video meetings where your face is prominently displayed, do not force others to take a second glance at you to see if the photo on your LinkedIn® profile is actually you. This need for a vanity security blanket to clutch onto those favorite photos of yourself is actually doing you a disservice. The best way to establish trust online is to make sure your professional photo *accurately* represents what you look like within at least the last two years.

Having grown up in this digital age where personal social media profiles are no longer the exception, but the norm, Millennials and Gen Z'ers are much more familiar with the online deception known as "catfishing". Dictionary.com includes this word in its slang definition as "a person who assumes a false identity or personality on the internet, especially on social media websites, as to deceive, manipulate, or swindle." I am quite sure that the principal I described above did not intend to catfish anyone by still using a headshot photo from 20 years ago, but just the visual misrepresentation alone can lead to others not trusting you online. If you only have one chance to make a first impression (and photos tend to capture the eye first) be truthful in how you represent yourself online by uploading a current photo.

Another important feature to consider on your personal LinkedIn® profile is a horizontal background photo. For me, it's a branded photo that features my latest printed stories, but I have seen several profiles, especially those that work in the A/E/C industry, where people include a photo of their favorite project. Maybe it is a dynamic drone image or their favorite design rendering they completed. It could be something that has nothing to do with work at all, such as your favorite trail to hike. All of those things say something about you and provide another opportunity to differentiate yourself; they also give people viewing your profile one more connection point—another reason to want to talk to you and start a professional business relationship.

Another way to break ground on your personal LinkedIn® profile is to write your own headline or tagline. Previously on LinkedIn,® the headline feature would automatically insert your most current job title. Prior to starting my own business, my headline would have read "Marketing Manager at klipp architecture."

Since then, LinkedIn® updated this feature, allowing users the ability to personalize the headline, so that it more accurately reflects their personal brand. I encourage my clients to get creative with this portion of their profile since the tagline immediately follows their name whenever they share a LinkedIn® post or comment on an existing one. Since this tagline is part of your first impression, make it count!

There are several "philosophies" on what this headline should contain. Regardless of what you include, be sure to take advantage of this opportunity to insert your personal brand. One of the more recent trends is to list various qualifier-type words that describe what you like to do in your job, what makes you an expert in a certain field, or express the way you think or approach life.

For instance, my profile once read:

"Professional Writer | Digital Content Creator | Social Media Maven | Capturer of Moments"

For a consulting engineer, your profile might read something like:

"Problem-Solver | Water-Design Enthusiast | Detailed Researcher | Community Builder"

For a construction professional, it could read:

"Placemaker | Hands-On Learner | Builder | Safety Guru"

As LinkedIn's® features continue to evolve, so will the trends on how you describe yourself and build your personal brand. At this juncture, I want a clear, first-person statement that is all encompassing of what my services actually do for my clients in the design and construction industry, so my current headline reads:

"I get people to care about the impactful stories behind design and construction projects."

Another missed opportunity when building your personal brand on LinkedIn® is professional designations. You should consider including and highlighting your professional designations at the very top of your profile, where it is permanently attached to your name. Again, with that first impression, let people know how hard you have worked in your career to advance yourself. Don't force others to have to scroll through your entire profile just to find out if you are a Professional Engineer (PE) or not. You graduated from school, paid all this money to study for and receive a professional credential, took the test, and then passed it to earn that particular designation, so lead with that and be proud of what you have accomplished in your career. The best way to do this is right at the top of your personal profile. While in "Edit" mode on LinkedIn,® next to where you would input your last name, add a comma, then your designation, so it is permanently fixed to your full name.

In 2009, I judiciously studied for the Leadership in Energy and Environmental Design Accredited Professional exam to demonstrate my growing interest in the design and construction industry. At the time, not too many people passed the exam on their first attempt, so when I did so, I couldn't wait to share this career milestone. I made sure to include this designation on every business card and professional profile I could.

The next section of your LinkedIn® profile that you should always keep current is your position and name of the company you represent. This may sound elementary and quite obvious, but if this information is inaccurate or outdated, you are giving others a free pass not to trust you. I harken back to the story of the owner from Texas who, during the project interview and selection process, was looking up every single presenter on LinkedIn® as they were presenting live and taking notes about whether the information listed on LinkedIn® was accurate or not. If you are trying to convince a developer whom you have never met to grant you the opportunity to design a $50 million office building and you misrepresent the company you work for on a public network, why would that owner trust you with that prominent design? Be transparent online and set the foundation for a trusting professional relationship by simply including accurate, up-to-date information about yourself.

Once you have updated your initial LinkedIn® personal profile, take it a step further and actually define your personal brand in the "About" section on LinkedIn.® I am 100 percent guilty of just using this section as a regurgitation of my resume, without ever truly personalizing it. (Scan this QR code for a "Before and After" screenshot of my "About" section.)

Again, I rejected the notion for so long that I needed a personal brand. It wasn't until—after almost eight years as the owner of Business Rewritten—I had flooded all of my efforts into building my company's online brand that I realized I needed to refocus more of my time on my personal online brand.

In September 2021, I enrolled in the IndeCollective Fall 2021 cohort at the behest of a longtime former colleague, Catlin "Cat" O'Shaughnessy Coffrin. We had worked together at McGraw-Hill Construction in Washington, D.C. from 2008 to 2009, which consequently, was how I initially entered the design and construction industry. We worked in the research and marketing department, where we focused on the stories behind commercial construction projects.

Fast forward to the spring of 2021, when Cat reached out to me, as we had been "keeping tabs" on each other via our LinkedIn® connection, to recommend I enroll in this entrepreneurial, modern MBA for independents. At this point in my career and business ownership journey, I found myself not even at a plateau, but more like stuck in a rut, and I needed to find the joy again when it came to my business. I remember during orientation night still feeling a bit sluggish but determined to grow, no matter how difficult or uncomfortable it was.

One of the most impactful sessions was actually the presentation that Cat led, "Building Your Personal Brand," in October 2021. Through a series of stories, value propositions, and examples of purposeful personal brands, the proverbial light bulb went off in my head that forced me to exit my comfort zone and truly challenge myself to answer those daunting questions:

- What is my purpose?
- What impact do I make on others?
- How do I make others feel?

During her presentation, Cat unveiled three writing prompts that truly spoke to me.

1. "Three things I have discovered about myself in the past year are..."
2. "One thing everyone gets wrong about [industry/area of expertise] is..."
3. "The biggest risk I ever took was [x], and here is how it shaped me."

After Cat's presentation, I dedicated an entire morning to answering these writing prompts with the goal of rewriting the

"About" section on my LinkedIn® profile to reflect my personal brand. See below for the resulting narrative:

> *I write words that compel others to care about untold stories. My purpose is to help my clients discover, write, and share the real story behind every building façade.*
>
> *These stories, in both the vertical and horizontal built environment, come in all shapes and sizes and can be told through various mediums—from digital and social media content to one-minute "get me to care" videos and social media campaigns, to researched and impactful case studies and published articles.*
>
> *I produce the best outcomes for my clients at the intersection of transparency, strong communication, and personalized connections.*
>
> *My StrengthsFinder Top Five Themes: Strategic | Achiever | Activator | Focused | Disciplined*

Moving further down in your profile sequentially, the next section is the "Experience" section. As a rule of thumb, you do not need to list every single part-time job, internship, and/or full-time job you have ever had. I myself have had several jobs since graduating from the University of Maryland in 2003, but I only include the positions that I care about most and that support my personal brand. Again, be strategic in terms of what you share with others. You want to make sure that you are representing yourself professionally and that the information listed is the most relevant and up to date.

Following the "Experience" section are your "Education" and "Licenses and Credentials," which are pretty much self-explanatory. The next portion that should appear on your LinkedIn® profile is your "Volunteer" experience that highlights what you choose to do outside of work. We all have the same 24 hours in a day, and if the majority of people in the U.S. spend eight hours sleeping and eight hours working, what about the remaining eight hours? What you choose to do with your own time helps share a broader perspective about you as a person and what you care about. It also provides another connection point for someone who is scanning your profile to see if they have anything in common with you or something they can talk to you about beyond just, "Hey, what did you think of that design project?" Business development is based on the concept of mutually beneficial relationships and creating connections with people. If you only list your current position and nothing else on your profile, you are missing out on a whole community of people you could connect with to further develop your professional network.

As we continue to go through your personal LinkedIn® profile in this chapter, I can already feel your eyes glazing over and, perhaps, even putting down this book. I get it. It does take a considerable amount of time and effort to consider what you want to share with others in a professional environment. But, in the long run, it will really help you stand out and tell a better story of who you are as a professional and what your personal brand is. So, keep reading—only a few more sections to go.

The next section on your personal LinkedIn® profile is the "Skills and Endorsements" section. This is the section where you can really highlight the various skills that you are most proficient at. I know from having worked in-house at both an engineering firm and an architecture firm in marketing and business development roles, we are essentially responsible for everything. "Marketing" often times becomes a catch-all phrase that includes a myriad of skills and responsibilities within a firm—you need to maintain the website, keep up with proposal deadlines, write news releases, compose social media posts, and wear all of these different hats, so to speak. The same thing goes for professionals in general. There are a number of skills that you must first learn, then master, before being able to teach others, so include all of them on your LinkedIn® profile to demonstrate your breadth of knowledge.

Once you have identified your main skills and the best practices you have learned on the job, the next step is to actually be endorsed for those particular skills. As you can see from my own personal profile, at one point in time, proposal writing was my world! I can't even tell you how many hours of my life I've spent writing proposals and prepping interview teams, so it's still my "Top Skill" based on the number of people that have endorsed me for that particular skill. It definitely takes time to build up endorsements for the skills you list on your profile, but over time, it does give people a flavor and understanding of the various skills that you are most proficient at.

This next one is a "new-ish" feature on LinkedIn,® but could be another missed opportunity if users do not take advantage of it—the "Recommendations" section. These are essentially personal testimonials, which you can request from others to write about you, and in turn, you can write a recommendation for that person. Again, continue the theme of what business development truly is—MUTUALLY BENEFICIAL relationships. If someone takes the time to say what a resourceful person you are and how much they really enjoyed partnering with you, you need to return that favor and write a recommendation for that person, too.

This is where your peer-to-peer network can really shine and be used to your advantage. For example, as A/E/C professionals, we are often working on different project teams made up of people from different companies with various backgrounds. So, let's say you were on a job where the superintendent noticed that you showed up to the jobsite every day on time and you weren't afraid to deal with all of those Change Orders or Requests for Information (RFI's). You should ask that superintendent for a recommendation.

In this section on LinkedIn,® when you click on the pencil-like button, there is literally an option to select "Ask for a Recommendation." Click on that, then type in the name of the person you would like to request a recommendation from, and the system will send them a notification. Again, build on that foundation of business development where relationships are mutually beneficial. If you ask someone for a recommendation, please return that favor and send one to that person in return. They may or may not necessarily want a recommendation from you, and that's okay. But by extending the offer, or even sending one that the receiving person may not even post on their profile, it shows that you are willing to be reciprocal. And perhaps, instead of writing a recommendation in return, you are able to help that particular person in a different capacity. Just remember to always acknowledge the favor and be willing to do something in return for that person. It establishes a sense of accountability for both of you—in that you are willing to do what you say you're going to do—and, thereby, lays the foundation of trust in your business development relationships.

Following the "Recommendations" section is the "Honors and Awards" portion of your LinkedIn® personal profile. Not everyone has received specific professional recognition, but if you have, make sure you include it. I understand some people want to be humble and not be labeled as boastful, but being upfront and honest about what you have accomplished in your career does not directly equate to arrogance, but more to transparency. It is another piece to your personal online brand that demonstrates your ability to go above and beyond.

One of the last sections on your personal LinkedIn® profile is the "Organizations" section, where you can include the professional associations and organizations that you participate in, whether that's just as a member, an active committee volunteer, or even a board position. This helps demonstrate how active you are in your particular industry and how you spend your time outside of work. I typically scroll to this section first when I initially search for a particular individual to see if we have mutual interests and if I will possibly see them at an upcoming industry event if we belong to the same organization. It helps me plan my networking opportunities and establishes another connection point between myself and that person.

Coming back full circle from initially avoiding a personal brand, to accepting the need for a personal brand, to then being strategic about creating a personal brand are all in the realm of possibility with your personal LinkedIn® profile. By being an active and engaged participant on LinkedIn,® you are already breaking ground on your personal brand and sharing it with others.

Get on LinkedIn,® Section 2

Now that you have broken ground on your personal profile and have a better understanding of all the ways you can build your personal brand, it's time to get on LinkedIn® and make some updates.

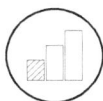

Novice = Add one of the "Recommended" sections to your profile according to LinkedIn,® which include the following types of information:

- Featured = Post a recent article you have written, a link to a website you have built, or project you have just completed.
- Licenses and certifications = Include your professional designations here and specific certifications you have received throughout your career.
- Courses = List a course of study you took in school—graduate or post-graduate level—that made a significant impact on your life.
- Recommendations = Send an invite to one of your colleagues asking them to write a personal recommendation for you that you can post on your LinkedIn® profile.

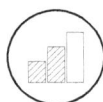

Intermediate = Add one or more of the "Additional" sections that LinkedIn® provides for your personal profile.

- Volunteer experience = Share which organizations you are passionate about supporting and how this volunteer experience has made a difference in your life or the lives of others.
- Publications = Include some of the latest articles or papers you have authored to include the headline, subject matter, publication name, and URL.
- Patents = Are you responsible for an existing or pending patent? Show others how innovative you are.

- Projects = Include milestones and results from some of the latest projects you have worked on.
- Honors and Awards = Allow others to see how your colleagues or industry partners have recognized you in some way.
- Test Scores = I actually do not recommend this section to my clients because a number is just a number and does not always tell the full story about your skill level.
- Languages = If you are gifted enough to speak multiple languages fluently, that could open more doors of opportunity for you. Make sure you include this information.
- Organizations = Include the associations or working groups you actively participate in, along with any particular role that you serve in and an explanation of why you are involved in that organization.

Experienced = Add a new section to your profile for "Providing Services" [NOTE: Do this regardless of whether you are a consultant or full-time employee] and create your own personalized services page that supplements your personal profile.

- On your personal LinkedIn® profile, click on "Open To," select "Providing Services," and then create a services page that includes a short intro bio, the skills/services you are best at, and media files (images) for examples. This helps to establish and build your personal brand on LinkedIn® by highlighting what you like to do and providing a visual representation of your career through the media files and examples you provide.

SET THE FOUNDATION TO BE A TRUSTED RESOURCE

3

TALKS ABOUT:
#TrustedResource #BuildTrust #TransparencyOnline

Once you have broken ground on your LinkedIn® profile and started to build your personal brand, the next step is to set the foundation to become a trusted resource for others.

What is a Trusted Resource?

We are all familiar with and have been inundated with online ads that are intended to build trust with a certain brand and may have even influenced you enough to share that sponsored post with your network. But how do we build trust with others for our personal brand without creating an advertisement that may be perceived as disingenuous or inauthentic? Furthermore, how do we influence others to share our personal brand without it turning into a shallow high school popularity contest? The simplest answer is by helping others.

Throughout my 14 years of social media marketing, with 11 of those years focused on LinkedIn,® one of the most overlooked opportunities for professionals is helping others online in order to build trusted relationships. Figuring out who you are as a professional and sharing that information on your LinkedIn® profile is only part of the equation to build trust. You then need to take it a step further to actually engage with others online. Sharing and posting relevant industry news, best practices to overcome a common workplace challenge, or even personal anecdotes about your career path and how you have grown as a professional are all ways to authentically become a trusted resource for others.

Another way to consider this notion of a trusted resource is by likening this concept to your circle of friends. There is usually one or two people in your group that you trust to confide in and ask for advice from whenever you are facing a challenging time in your life. What about this person allows you trust them? Most likely it is due to their ability to be open and available to you on a consistent basis. You may also take comfort in knowing that that particular person has experienced something similar to your challenge and found productive ways to overcome that issue. This friend may also offer relevant resources to you in the form of a community group to join or workout class to attend, helping you build your own toolbox of solutions to sustain you and help you grow as a person. Once you trust that friend to help you, you will most likely find yourself introducing that friend to others as well.

The same concept can be applied to your professional online presence and ability to be a trusted resource for your network of LinkedIn® connections. Although you may not have people reaching out to you directly on LinkedIn® asking for help, the very nature of LinkedIn® itself is that it is a SOCIAL network meant to connect people. Human beings are flawed, and we are all coping with our own set of issues that we may not feel comfortable enough to share publicly online. When you begin sharing relevant, helpful information via your personal profile on a consistent basis and respond to others' comments and questions, you begin to establish yourself as a trusted resource and have now set the foundation for mutually beneficial business relationships with others.

What to Post

Whenever I am hired on by my design and construction clients for online personal and company branding best practices, after answering the question of "Why do I need a profile?," the second most popular question I receive is, "What should I post?"

If you are still new to personal branding and sharing information online, I typically recommend starting out by sharing current industry news relevant to your area of expertise, or information about an online training or in-person networking event to inform others you are attending and to encourage them to register as well. This activity shows that not only are you engaged and have a pulse on the industry, but that you are constantly learning and willing to help others do the same. It also demonstrates that you take the time to receive continuing education and learn new processes. All of these things speak volumes about you as a person and your character, and they ultimately reflect your personal brand. Without even realizing it, you are helping others learn more about you, all while serving as a trusted resource for others.

Once you begin to post more consistently, you can then become more intentional with your posts by writing your own content to share. These kind of posts help others learn more about you and how you handle challenges in the workplace.

These internally-generated posts also help establish and reinforce your personal brand.

Externally-Generated Posts

One of the best ways to help you start posting on a regular basis is by sharing relevant content that has been generated by others. This low-hanging fruit can come in the form of a relevant industry article or simply by re-sharing a post from one of your LinkedIn® connections. As a Social Media Strategist, I typically share out the latest articles on social media best practices, content ideas, and social media research data. One way to establish yourself as an expert in whatever field you work in is to post relevant articles about your area of expertise on a consistent basis. These posts then become the building blocks of your personal brand, and they highlight industry topics that you care about.

Another external type of post is to send an event invite. Whenever you register for an industry-related event, create a post telling people that you are attending and share out the link for others to register. This not only shows that you are engaged in the industry you work in, but also that you, as a person, are taking the time to educate yourself and to receive training or continued education in order to advance in your career. It also shows that you are willing to engage in learning opportunities outside of your prescribed job role. Sharing an event invite on LinkedIn® also puts you in a favorable light to the organization that is hosting the event, since you are helping to spread the word about registration. If you are looking for a new job, this type of post can also make you more attractive to future employers on LinkedIn® who want to gather more information about who you are beyond just your current job title and company, and it gives them an idea of your interests and talents outside of the typical workday.

If you are still struggling with what to post, start sharing out articles and posts from your favorite industry associations. Use the "Search" function in LinkedIn® to identify relevant associations and groups on LinkedIn® that you can then follow in order to start seeing their updates in your personal news feed. When you come across a relevant post from your favorite organization, simply hit "Share" at the bottom of the post (or that arrow pointing to the right from your smartphone). This simple "Share" function from your favorite industry organization demonstrates that you are involved in that organization, that you care about what is going on in the industry, and that you are staying current on the latest trends.

Internally-Generated Posts

Once you are consistently sharing content and information originating from other sources, the next step is to start generating your own content to post on your LinkedIn® personal profile and share with your network of connections. If the thought of writing your own content to share publicly seems daunting or you are simply running out of ideas on what to post this week, a simple "thank you" post goes a long way.

For example, I recently completed a video project with a partnering company and shared a snippet of that video series in a LinkedIn® post as a thank you for everyone's hard work on the project. I took the time to not only say thank you to the partnering company's owner, who I worked with personally, but also to say thank you to Tony Milo, President and CEO of the Colorado Contractors Association, who was our client on that project. This simple gesture was a way to publicly acknowledge and thank Tony for not only providing us the opportunity to work on the videos, but also for trusting our vision. It also served as a way to share out an example of my latest work, and something that I am really proud of, in a way that didn't come off as, "Hey, look what I did." It was a show of gratitude to our client for giving us the opportunity to tell an impactful story in the construction industry.

Once you feel more comfortable with generating your own posts, you can then embrace your LinkedIn® personal profile as a platform to start revealing more aspects of your personal brand and how you can help others. There are many schools of thought about the various kinds of subject matter to write about and share on LinkedIn,® from the unspoken mandate to keep the content "professional," to breaking down all barriers and posting whatever is at the forefront of your stream of consciousness. We could debate about both ends of the spectrum with pluses and minuses, but the real answer is to share the kind of content that is most in line with your personal brand.

For instance, if you are a veterinarian and your passion project is saving felines who have been abandoned in downtown alleyways, then cat photos and those rescue stories are more than appropriate for your overall theme of LinkedIn® personal posts. However, haphazardly posting cat photos with no context on your LinkedIn® profile can be off-putting to your connections and may cause you to lose some followers, who would most likely prefer that you post those cat photos on a "less professional" social network. It might also cause others not to trust you and leave them confused about your personal brand.

As a rule of thumb, I recommend that my clients consider the answers to the below questions before writing and sharing a personal post on LinkedIn.®

1. Is this subject matter relevant to my current position or to a future role I would like to play in a particular industry? OR, does the subject matter reflect one of my personal passion projects that I care deeply about?

2. By sharing this particular story, could others benefit from my lessons learned?
3. Would I feel comfortable sharing this story with a colleague of mine at the office or at an industry event?

In addition to the answers to the above questions, also consider what your end goal is with this personal post. What kind of impact do you want to make on your connections? For instance, are you aiming to educate others about a common industry problem or perhaps highlight an unsung hero who has helped you in your career? Do you want others to then share their own personal story that relates to yours? If so, you cannot simply post your own story and then walk away. In order for others to feel comfortable sharing their stories, you should engage with people who leave "Comments" on your post and ask follow up questions or perhaps share an online resource that helped you.

One recent example of a post that reflects my personal brand was short and sweet but contained an overall larger message about how women are treated in the workplace. As a professional, working hard to establish my credibility as a writer, marketer, and business developer in the construction industry—where women only represent about 12 percent of the total workforce—many of my male counterparts and/or higher-ranking executives have focused too much of their attention on my smile. From being told that I need to "smile more" so that others will listen to me, or to "smile less" because no one will take me seriously, I find myself in a no-win situation. Without blatantly saying that I constantly battle with and thwart chauvinistic behavior to demonstrate my ability to be a trusted resource, I simply embraced my smile and ability to spread joy by posting the following:

I can't tell you how many times in my career I have been told to:

1. *"Smile MORE, honey"*
2. *"Smile less, or no one will take you seriously"*

In the end, you will always lose when you value other's opinions more than your own personal brand and business strategy.

#SpreadJoy

"No one is you and that is your superpower" ~ Brian Ford #QOTD

This post received over 3,400 "Impressions" and generated several comments that I responded back to individually. It opened the door for other women to share their experiences and also garnered support from my personal network to embrace what makes each of us unique. (Scan this QR code to view this post and the results.)

Not every post on your profile needs to be this intentional, but the sum of your posts should equal your personal brand, reflecting what you have experienced as a professional and demonstrating how you can use your platform to be a trusted resource for others.

Get on LinkedIn,® Section 3

Now that you have created a rock star personal profile and you are well on your way to becoming a professional business developer, you actually have to post on LinkedIn.® Below are some basic tips and tricks on how and what to post, so you can demonstrate your personal brand—all while providing value to others as a trusted resource.

Novice = Share a relevant research study from an industry association that you belong to.

1. Use the "Search" function in the upper left-hand corner of the LinkedIn® platform to find your industry association's LinkedIn® page.
2. Scroll down through the library of posts and find a recent post (within the past few weeks) that provides helpful research data points for a common industry problem.
3. Click "Share" and be sure to add a sentence or two about why you are sharing this post. For instance, you can type:

> *"#DYK (Did you know) that 76 percent of Gen Z'ers are looking for a career path, not just a job, where they can make a social impact. How will you incorporate this into your company's recruiting efforts?"*

Intermediate = Share an example of a project that you completed and how it benefited others.

1. Create a graphic representing your project or, better yet, a video highlight reel that captures the project's overall intent, challenges, and solutions.
2. Share that graphic or video as a personal post with a headline that grabs people's attention, a snippet of

how your project impacted others, and a link for people to learn more.

3. Monitor people's reactions and comments on your post, responding in kind to any follow-up questions people leave, or simply just "Liking" their comments.

Experienced = Share a personal, vulnerable story about a challenge you faced at work and how it helped you grow as a professional.

1. Include relevant photos or perhaps a video of an interview from a podcast that you spoke on that reflects your feelings on this story.

2. Include a detailed account of the challenge, how it impacted your career, and what the end result included.

3. This level of vulnerability in a professional setting, while scary for some, actually allows others to relate to you more and creates deeper roots of trust between you and others as it demonstrates that you are a trusted resource who is not afraid to share personal stories of struggle.

BUILD OUT YOUR PERSONAL BUSINESS DEVELOPMENT NETWORK

4

As you read in Chapter 1 of this book, entitled "Invest in Yourself," the oxygen mask metaphor prescribed that before you can be a trusted resource and connector for others, you must invest in yourself to create and protect your personal online brand. Now that you are nearing the end of "Section 1: Personal LinkedIn® Branding," my hope for you is that you have made some tangible updates and enhancements to your personal LinkedIn® profile, such as: a compelling "About" statement that highlights your greatest strengths and describes how you best perform; personal recommendations you have garnered from others; a full description of your volunteer passion projects; and inclusion of all of your professional designations at the top of your profile, just to name a few. Now that you have created this profile and have framed out your professional network, it is time to shift gears and actually DO some business development.

The ultimate question, then, is: What is business development?

Business development (BD) has assumed several connotations over the years in various industries, from a purely sales and numbers-driven vantage point to describing an entire 360-degree mantra on how to interact with others. In my 20 years of marketing and business development experience, I find that, all too often, BD professionals and entrepreneurs rely on a numbers-driven sales strategy to form relationships with potential clients, with the end goal of winning a project for their company.

There is nothing wrong with this strategy, and it can be profitable for firms based on the Return on Investment (ROI) reporting for that particular quarter or year. However, in this transactional type of relationship—where the BD professional or entrepreneur is only seeking more projects and is not offering anything of value in return for that potential client—the relationship becomes one-sided and typically has a start date when the project is secured and an end date when the project is turned over to the owner. (Scan the QR code for additional visual resources.)

This strategy performs well in the short-term under ideal circumstances, when business is booming and the economy is steady. But what happens when a global pandemic brings business to a striking halt for a period of time or when an international war breaks out that affects the supply chain of materials or simply if your superstar client decides to work with another service provider? What is your long-term strategy to mitigate these unknowns in business and create a steady flow of opportunities regardless of external conditions? The answer lies in building mutually beneficial business relationships as the foundation of your firm's business development strategy. Or simply put, by helping others succeed, you succeed as well.

Another way to consider this BD notion of mutually beneficial relationships is that, at the end of the day, people like working with people they like. Maya Angelou, renowned author, stated it best when she said, "People will forget what you *said*, people will forget what you *did*, but people will never forget how you made them *feel*." When you help others solve a problem or support them through a difficult time, you form a bond with that particular person and have hopefully made them feel positive about your relationship. Building a relationship based on problem-solving for each other sets a firm foundation for a long-term, mutually beneficial business development strategy.

But how can you develop these mutually beneficial relationships online? This is, again, where LinkedIn® can support your business development efforts. Let me reinforce this notion— LinkedIn® is a free tool that you can use to your advantage, but it takes time, effort, and consistency. Once you learn how to navigate LinkedIn® and all of its different features, LinkedIn® can be a very effective tool to augment your overall business development strategy.

Let's start with the basics, or rather the low-hanging fruit. As I mentioned earlier, your personal profile is essentially your digital business card. From 2020–2021, when most of the business community was confined to interacting with others via video calls online, I received several complaints from my clients that business development was nearly impossible during a time when there were no major in-person conferences, no industry events, and not even in-person coffee meetings, which were always my favorite go-to when I was building my professional network. Although most of these restrictions are in our rearview for now, we still need to incorporate an online BD mentality into our overall business development strategy to execute a more hybrid approach.

One way that I continued to build my professional network when I found myself stuck on Zoom® meetings all day was to be curious and find out who else was stuck in Zoom® jail with me in our squares. For instance, whenever I joined a Zoom® meeting/presentation, I first scanned the list of participants to ascertain, do I know any of them? Am I directly connected with that person on LinkedIn®? Do I share a mutual connection or point of interest with that person? If I answered no to any of those questions, I would search LinkedIn® with that person's first and last name, send a connection request to that person, and include a note saying something like, "Hi Byron, I saw that you were also on the Prevailing Wage seminar this morning. I hope you found it valuable. I would love to connect and learn more about you and your firm." And boom, you just increased your professional network simply by sitting in on another Zoom® meeting.

Another tactic I like to use is, if I am the one leading and/or hosting a Zoom® call, I start off the meeting by having everyone copy and paste the link to their personal LinkedIn® profile into the chat. This way, you are able to "exchange business cards" digitally and, again, increase your business development network just by showing up. You can also take it a step further and have the LinkedIn® profile exchange serve as a digital "icebreaker"—where you can go around to each person on Zoom® and share a fun fact about yourself that is NOT on your profile. So instead of just saying your name, company, and title, you can provide another connection point for others to connect with you. For instance, I often introduce myself as, "Hi, I'm Julie Wanzer, owner of Business Rewritten. I've lived in Colorado for over 10 years, and I don't ski, but I love the mountains." This usually sparks some kind of "debate" about the Rocky Mountains and encourages others to share a fun fact and offer a connection point.

Now that we've exchanged our digital business cards and you have made a new connection on LinkedIn®—or several of them—you will now start to receive notifications about that particular person. This is the best way to start learning more about your clients, your peers, and others you are connected to. These notifications typically include job anniversaries, a new title or promotion, or notifications about posts that particular person is tagged in from other people's posts. LinkedIn® most recently added a notification that when you sign up for a conference or an event, that notification is now sent out to your entire network. You are able to share what you are doing professionally via your profile and your activity, without having to personally reach out to your network one by one.

For instance, as I was scrolling through my notifications, I saw that Chad Holtzinger was celebrating his nine-year anniversary as the founder of Shopworks. This prompted me to reach out and send him a message via LinkedIn® that read, "Wow, Chad, I haven't seen you in a while. Congratulations on your founder-anniversary! The last time I saw you was at the Housing Colorado conference almost three years ago, and I would love to hear more about what you're doing now with your company." It was a simple message but served as a critical connection point and reason to follow up with him. Certainly, much has happened since 2019, and it gave me an excuse to reach out to Chad, without it feeling like a "cold call" or entirely random. This practice also demonstrates that I am taking an interest in Chad and gives me a jumping off point for our next conversation and/or meet-up. The best part is that all of these notifications are already built into LinkedIn® for you. You do not have to create a separate notification in your Outlook® or Google® calendar to remind you of your potential clients' career milestones. These LinkedIn® notifications provide the BD breadcrumbs you need to create connection points that will help nurture your business development relationships.

In addition to the LinkedIn® people notifications, another business development tactic that you can take advantage of on LinkedIn® is using the "Search" function to "do your people research." In an article I wrote, which was published by the Associated General Contractors of America's *Constructor Magazine* in September 2021, I emphasized the importance of reconnecting with people as the basis of business development strategies as the nation returned to the office.

The article focused on the premise that before you can be a trusted resource for your professional connections, you need to do your homework about the people you are working with, from your clients to *potential* clients to colleagues, and even mentors.

Below is an excerpt from the article:

Business Development Best Practices to Reconnect as the Nation Returns to the Office

Business development (BD) in the construction industry is a continual building and rebuilding of mutually beneficial relationships. Although this practice of building and rebuilding relationships was surely tested over the past year, BD professionals still found unique and creative ways to connect. Whether that was through a LinkedIn® virtual leads group or setting records for the greatest number of video meetings in one day, BD professionals certainly adopted their practices to fit the needs of their clientele.

As we are called on to shift our business practices during this "return to the office" boom, BD professionals must once again find creative ways to reconnect with clients and also connect with new ones. Based on your clients' levels of comfortability, consider these best practices to re-engage and rebuild.

1. Do Your People Research: It goes without saying that this past year has brought about many changes in both people's professional and personal lives. Several long-term professionals retired, others transitioned to another construction or A/E/C industry firm, some people moved across the nation to be closer to family, and others left the construction industry altogether.

Start by mining your LinkedIn® connections to find out which firms your clients are currently working at, and take note of any profile updates like:

- *Did they receive a promotion in the past year?*
- *Are they pursuing their own business venture now?*
- *Did they start volunteering for a cause they are passionate about?*

Most of us have not had recent, active experience with speaking face to face with clients, so take the time to prepare and relearn how to engage with the person you would like to sit across from you.

2. Say Thank You: Once you have done your people research, start categorizing your list of clients to identify:

- *Who have you worked closely with over the past year, but have not connected with in a while?*
- *Who have you NOT worked with over the past year, and need to reconnect with?*
- *Who do you WANT to work with over this coming year, and how can you either meet that person, or find a mutual connection point?*

If you are having a difficult time figuring out what to even say to your clients, start with "Thank you." It is never too late to say thank you and reach out to that professional contact for supporting you and your firm. By reaching out and scheduling that thank you lunch or happy hour, not only can you "properly" thank that person for remaining a client, but also learn more about how this past year affected them both professionally and personally. Sometimes just listening is the best way to reconnect with someone and show them you are generally interested in their professional development.

These thank you interactions can also be an opportunity to learn about future projects during the course of your conversation without directly asking "What is your next project and how can I be a part of it?" Some examples of leading questions to ask for future business include:

- *What are you looking forward to most over the summer? Or in the fall?*
- *How will you do business differently moving forward?*
- *What did you miss most when we were actively working together?*

One of the most frequently asked questions I receive when working with individuals to build their BD network on LinkedIn® is, "How do I grow my network, and who should I connect with?" And I have a two-part answer.

1. Be intentional.
2. Connect with potential clients, current clients, partners, colleagues, and personal allies that can connect you with others.

To expand on that part one answer, my recommendation is to first be intentional about how you want to grow your list of connections. The advice I give to my clients is to focus more on the quality of your connections versus quantity. Yes, having 10,000 followers may impress some people, but can you identify all of the connection points that you have with each of those 10,000 people? Can you trust that if you reach out to someone on your follower list, they will actually respond to you? Remember, the basis of business development is to create mutually beneficial relationships that will win you more work. Focus your time and energy more on the quality of your connections and the rapport you have built with them as a trusted resource, rather than just adding to your follower list.

With a mindset focused on the quality of your LinkedIn® connections, let's take a deeper dive into how you can actually build your following. I recommend that my clients first develop a target list of companies that fit their ideal client profile. Consider not only the typical demographics of your desired clientele, such as industry type, market size, and location, but also more personal qualifiers, such as communication style, passion projects, and common pain points.

Then, use LinkedIn's® "Search" function to type in the name of those particular companies and start to follow their LinkedIn® company pages. From there, investigate further to identify the individuals that work at the particular company that you would like to be connected with. For people you are not currently connected to, but would like to reach out to, begin by scanning their personal profiles to find some point of connection. I typically start with some basic characteristics to answer the following questions:

- Have I worked at the same firm as this person, but at different times?
- Did we attend the same college or master class program?
- Do we volunteer for the same organization or same kind of nonprofit?
- Has this person published an article in a publication I follow and enjoy?

Once I have found a connection point, I then send that person a "Connect" request with a message via LinkedIn® that includes our mutual connection point and ask to learn more about them. I would note that not everyone on LinkedIn® is necessarily active on LinkedIn,® so do not lose hope when someone does not respond back to you immediately. You are building a network, and it takes time. If that person rejects your request or never responds back, then they are not worth connecting with anyway. Time to move on to the next connection point.

For people that you are already connected to but have not spoken with or seen in quite some time, there are still plenty of reasons to reach out to them. Following this era of the "Great Resignation," people have changed jobs, titles, industries, and even moved across the country. I set a quarterly reminder on my calendar to go through my entire list of LinkedIn® connections, so I can consistently stay up to date on my professional network. In doing so, I typically find several reasons to reach out to people—whether that is to congratulate them for that promotion they just received or to celebrate a work anniversary, starting a new company, going back to school, or completing a master class, like IndeCollective.

My list of followers includes several of my clients, potential clients, colleagues, former bosses, and even some of my competitors, because you never know who in your network will end up serving as a resource for you or even a referral. Diversifying your network of connections helps you to be a resource for others and, in turn, helps you build out your personal BD network.

Get on LinkedIn,® Section 4

Armed with some insights on how to build out your personal business development network, now it's time to actually get on LinkedIn® and start implementing these practices as part of your overall business development strategy.

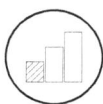

Novice = Obtain a list of your current company staff and make sure you are personally connected to each employee. Use the "Search" function to identify each person, then send a "Connect" request. Just by searching for each individual and scanning their profiles, you can learn something new about that person and find another connection point. Perhaps someone you work with currently used to work for your dream company or also volunteers at the same organization that you do, but you have yet to cross paths or attend the same event. Connecting with people that you currently work with helps to increase your overall network and allows you to get to know them better.

Intermediate = Once you register for an upcoming conference, take the time to scan the list of speakers and attendees (if available) and reach out to each person individually to connect with them. For these connections, since you most likely have never met them before, include a personal message to the effect of:

> "I saw that you are speaking at the upcoming Digicon conference, and I'm looking forward to attending your session. It would be great to make a new connection at the conference."

You could even follow up with that person once you are connected, to ask if they have time to meet to discuss best practices regarding their talk or to learn more about each other's businesses and how you could possibly help each other.

Experienced = Extend business development strategies to your firm's recruiting program and involve more people in the hiring process to vet out a potential good fit for your company. Once you receive a resume for a potential new employee, review that person's LinkedIn® profile and see if there are mutual connections with anyone who currently works at your firm. Then reach out to that person and inquire about what it's like to work with that person, what their personality is like, or how that person reacts under pressure.

This can also be applied to interview prep for your project teams. Once you find out who is on the selection committee for an upcoming project interview, do your people research and find out more about those interview committee members. Do you have any mutual connections with that person? Do you share the same interests? Use their profiles to find some common ground between your project team and the selection committee, so you can establish a rapport with that committee member and help tell a more convincing story as to why they should select your firm's team for the project.

Before we take a deeper dive into LinkedIn® company page best practices, here are some frequently asked questions about personal profiles. They cover what to post and other personal business development tricks you can master via LinkedIn.®

Q: **I do not work in our company's marketing department and want to share various articles from other companies and organizations. Should I check with our internal marketing department before sharing certain posts?**

A: *As an employee of a firm, you are an extension of that company's brand, and you should have a critical eye as to what you share out via your personal LinkedIn.® You can certainly share out issues that you personally care about, but be professional. LinkedIn® is not a hosting ground for political or religious views. It is a social platform of business professionals.*

If you are still hesitant as to what to post from outside your organization, start with just sharing or reposting relevant posts from your company's LinkedIn® company page. These posts have already been "cleared" via your company's marketing department and are "safe" to share.

Q: I seem to only receive notifications and messages from headhunters on LinkedIn.® Does that group of people use LinkedIn® more than anyone?

A: *My immediate response is that you are most likely not sharing enough content about yourself on LinkedIn® and not serving as a resource to others. If you only have a profile because someone in your marketing department set it up for you, then yes, you will most likely only receive messages from headhunters who want something from you.*

Keep in mind, this is not a bad thing—especially if you are looking for a new job.

For a longer answer, you are correct—LinkedIn® was originally used by Human Resources and headhunters to find people based on their title and company and offer them something better. If you are not looking for a position, I would block those people's messages or select "I don't know this person" when a headhunter is trying to connect with you.

Q: I often see people with a LinkedIn® gold logo on their profile. What does that mean, and how do I get one?

A: *The gold emblem logo designates that that person has paid for a LinkedIn® Premium account. This type of account includes more connection features and allows you to collect more data about people, companies, and trends. I signed up for the 30-day trial and did not find much use for it. For the amount of money LinkedIn® wanted for me to be a premium member, it did not seem worth the value I was getting out of it. To me, LinkedIn® should remain a free network, open to all who follow the platform's guidelines.*

[NOTE: I can see the value if you are an HR professional or headhunter, because it does allow for more detailed searches and access to more data.]

Q: **How do you handle opposition from leadership to posting on LinkedIn®?**

A: *Opposition to posting seems to walk the line between personal and professional values. My answer is that you have to meet your company's leadership team somewhere in the middle.*

Again, I go back to that story of the owner who was sitting in on these project interviews and making decisions about principals at these firms who had been in the industry for 30+ years. If they did not even have a LinkedIn® profile, the owner was immediately dismissive of that person because he couldn't access any information about them or readily see who else they were connected to that the owner might know and contact after the project interview to find out what that person is really like to work with. Don't lose work over not having a LinkedIn® profile.

Also, kindly remind your leadership that in this era of digital information, almost anyone can find out personal information about you with a few clicks online. LinkedIn® is a social network that includes people from several different generations, backgrounds, and certainly, personal philosophies. Your LinkedIn® profile is your platform to show others what you care about, your personal expertise, and how you interact with others in the industry.

PART

COMPANY
LinkedIn®
BRANDING

SHIFT GEARS FROM PERSONAL BRANDING TO COMPANY BRANDING

Now that you have established yourself personally on LinkedIn,® it is time to shift gears to focus on company branding online. I can honestly admit that writing this part of the book was much easier for me because, as a Marketing Professional, I have been branding companies since 2003, when I first entered the workforce after graduating with a B.S. in Marketing from the University of Maryland's Robert H. Smith School of Business.

Marketing and branding principles have certainly evolved over the years and include so many more mediums through which you can build a company's brand—each with its own nuances. For instance, although both websites and social media are considered "online" mediums, best practices in branding a company on its own website versus best practices in branding a company on LinkedIn® do, in fact, vary greatly.

Another way to conceptualize this is to consider the different ways in which you communicate via your smart phone. Think about the nuances in how your communication differs when you call someone versus when you text someone. The message can be exactly the same to notify someone that you are outside their house and ready to go, and you are using the same medium, your smart phone, but the message you would leave on someone's voicemail versus the message in a text can vary greatly.

Part II of this book focuses on company branding on LinkedIn,® but it takes the concept a step further, to demonstrate not only how to brand the company, but also how to become a trusted brand. The August 2021 study by PwC called "The Complexity of Trust: PwC's Trust in US Business Survey"[4] found that:

- "49 percent of consumers have started or increased purchases from a company because they trust it.
- 33 percent of consumers have paid a premium for trust.
- 44 percent of consumers have stopped buying from a company due to lack of trust.
- 22 percent of employees have left a company because of trust issues.
- 19 percent of employees have chosen to work at a company because they trusted it highly."

The question then remains, how do you build that trust with both your clients and your employees? The PwC survey found that the "top choices for drivers of trust among consumers were accountability, clear communications, and admitting mistakes."

The underlying message here is that to become a trusted brand, the company needs to do what it says it is going to do and communicate that message clearly in a public forum.

Strategic, consistent posting on LinkedIn® company pages provides that transparency and serves as the building blocks of trust to help tell the story of who you are as a firm and how the company wants to be represented online.

---

[4] SOURCE: PwC "The Complexity of Trust: PwC's Trust in US Business Survey" August 2021. https://www.pwc.com/us/en/library/trust-in-business-survey.html.

INVEST IN YOUR COMPANY: DIGITAL COMPANY BRANDING

5

:..:
TALKS ABOUT:
#DigitalContent #BuildTrust #FirmCulture
:..:

Since the dawn of the internet age in the 1990s, companies have developed a plethora of digital branding strategies in order to be found online and set themselves apart from their competitors. Company websites are typically one of the first branding projects implemented, but given the competitive online landscape for websites, increased usage of smart phones, and the growing dependence on smart phone apps, websites are simply not enough.

Consider the following:

In 1998, when Google® first debuted its search engine service, there were approximately 2.4 million websites on the

World Wide Web.[5] As of the most recent count of active websites in 2018, there are almost 1.5 billion websites—each competing for Google's® top rankings based on keyword searches.

Although there are many schools of thought regarding search engine optimization (SEO) tactics and how to elevate your company's website to meet Google's® ever-evolving algorithm, several SEO specialists and website developers agree that there are both technical and non-technical factors to consider. The top ranking factors typically include domain names, high quality consistent content, the number of backlinks (links that direct the user to another site), and social media tie-ins.

Beyond rebuilding your company's entire website with new links, the remaining factors you can influence are production of digital content and your company's social media activity. If you have ever worked in-house in a company's marketing and/or business development department, updating your company's website on a regular basis often involves several layers of approval. These can include the marketing staff, who will most likely generate the content to project managers that can supply relevant information to the final approval from either the vice president of marketing or the owner of the company to the IT department, who will monitor the website once these updates go live and mitigate any site failures. This process may take weeks or even months to complete, especially since website maintenance is not typically billable work, or other proposal-driven deadlines may take priority over the list of site updates that need to be made.

Other factors to consider when building an effective digital branding strategy include the increasing amount of time people are spending on their smart phones and the growing

---

[5] Source: Internet Live Stats, accessed July 18, 2022. https://www. internetlivestats.com/total-number-of-websites/.

dependence on smart phone apps. According to the *Digital 2022: Global Overview Report*,[6] global users spend an average of four hours and 48 minutes of each day using their smart phones. Of those nearly five hours, 92.5 percent of that time is spent using mobile apps while only 7.5 percent of that time is spent using web browsers on their smart phones. In addition, internet users are spending an average of two hours and 27 minutes on social media alone.

The message here is that if someone wants to access information, they are most likely doing so from their smart phone, via an app, rather than a browser—and most likely via a social media app. This drives home the point that if people are searching for information about your company, they are most likely using a social media app, like LinkedIn,® accessed from their smart phone. Since people are already actively scrolling through LinkedIn,® posting updates to your company page will increase the likelihood of others viewing those updates in their social media feed. Consistent posting essentially creates a one-stop shop where people can learn more about your company, its culture, and its people. In order to control the narrative and tell an impactful story about your company, your firm needs an active LinkedIn® company page where you are consistently posting quality content.

Why Company LinkedIn® Pages?

When working with marketing teams on their digital content and branding strategies on LinkedIn,® I often hear the question, "Why do we even need a company page? We already have a website." My response is to relate the old adage,

---

[6] Source: Digital 2022: Global Overview Report, DataReportal & We Are Social & Hootsuite, https://datareportal.com/reports/digital-2022-global-overview-report.

"If a tree falls in a forest and no one is around to hear it, does it make a sound?" Technically, the answer is that the falling of the tree does create sound waves, but if no human is there to receive those sound waves, there is no verifiable sound. Meaning, if you post an update on your company's website—perhaps about an award your company won—is that one update being received by your ideal audience and truly making an impact?

I then follow up with more questions to my client, including the following:

> *Beyond the standard website metrics of page visits and time spent on a page, how are you tracking exactly how many people saw this specific update?*

> *Did this update that includes important information influence the reader to actually implement your desired Call To Action (CTA) on your website?*

Without a technical coding background, you may never know the answers to these questions. My solution to these dilemmas is instead, to post these updates to your company's LinkedIn® page where you can take a deeper dive into LinkedIn's® company page "Analytics." These data points allow you to track how many views that one post received, how many people clicked on the CTA link, who the specific people are that commented or engaged directly with that post, and how many people shared that one post with their network of connections, which thereby increases the number of people viewing your original post.

Another way to drive home the message to your company's owners, principals, and chief marketing officers that your firm needs to be on LinkedIn® is that, of all the social media channels currently available, LinkedIn® is rated the number one social media channel for content marketing[7] in the B2B realm. Content marketing is critical because:

> *"it answers your audience's questions and helps you build trust, develop relationships, improve conversions, and generate leads."*[8]

With this in mind, how does this translate to your company's LinkedIn® page? It means that you should be posting those published articles written by members of your firm or sharing out those company award announcements, a snippet of a paper that one of your Project Managers recently wrote, or even better, a one-minute video from a presentation that one of your firm's principals recently completed. These are all examples of relevant content that you should be posting on your firm's LinkedIn® company page to drive home the message that your firm truly is an industry expert. (Scan QR code for visual infographic.)

Another important statistic to pay attention to is that 82 percent of B2B marketers find their greatest success with content marketing on LinkedIn.® You never want to feel like you are posting into a void, with no way to monitor your results or to feel like your time has been wasted in producing worthwhile content. As opposed to platforms like Twitter, where only 67 percent of marketers have found success, on LinkedIn,® your content marketing efforts go further and are much more likely to be seen and read by your intended audience.

---

[7] Source: Sophisticated Marketers' Guide to LinkedIn, 2020.

[8] Source: Hubspot, "10 Benefits of Consistent, High-Quality Content Marketing", https://blog.hubspot.com/marketing/benefits-high-quality-content-consistency-brand#:~:text=Why%20is%20content%20marketing%20important,content%20from%20their%20favorite%20brands.

Benefits of Posting to the LinkedIn® Company Page

Now that you have at least conceded that your company's website and the updates you are making to your site are not enough, you can now step into action and take advantage of all the benefits of having an established LinkedIn® company page. One benefit is to use your company page as a way to establish your firm as an industry expert. We all know that the design and construction industry is riddled with firms in each discipline—from mechanical and electrical engineering firms to structural to civil and landscape architecture (just to name a few of the consulting design disciplines, not including the variety of firms that specialize in each building sector). The questions remain: What makes your firm stand out? Why would someone want to come work for your firm? Or why would another design and construction team want to partner with you for an upcoming project? If you are consistently and strategically posting on your company's LinkedIn® page, you have already answered all of those questions.

Another benefit of a company LinkedIn® page is that it can serve as an extension of your firm's retainment and recruitment processes. There is no denying that most people are still primarily using LinkedIn® as a platform to look for new jobs. Amidst the "Great Resignation" or "Great Attrition," more than 4.2 million people have voluntarily quit their jobs as of May 2022, as compared to 3.8 million in May 2021, according to the U.S. Bureau of Labor Statistics (BLS). The number of job openings has also increased to 11.3 million in May 2022, as compared to 9.6 million in May 2021, per the BLS.

As a possible solution to this nationwide retainment issue, McKinsey & Company reported in March 2022 that employers must redefine their attraction and retention strategies to build a value proposition for employees. McKinsey concedes that competitive compensation is important, but "once that threshold has been met, cultural factors can make a company more attractive to join and, ideally, provide more incentive to stay."[9]

One way to demonstrate your company's culture online is via your LinkedIn® company page, where you can help tell that story and show that your firm values volunteerism, that your employees engage with each other off the jobsite, and that your firm is working on impactful design and construction projects. Post those photos from ground-breaking ceremonies, topping off parties, and other design and construction milestones to your company's LinkedIn® page. You can also post your annual report or corporate social responsibility (CSR) report on your LinkedIn® page. It helps convey that your company is transparent and willing to share information with others.

In addition to displaying your firm's culture to support your retainment and recruitment efforts, an active company page on LinkedIn® can also be used to target the next generation of the workforce. Job posting sites, like Indeed® and others, do not tell the full story of a company or why someone might want to work there. LinkedIn® allows job seekers to gain a more holistic view of the company they want to work for, including who currently works at the company, who, if anyone, the job seeker is connected to at that company, what kind of employee activities the company hosts, and when the last time was that the company received media coverage.

This profile also helps to tell the story of a firm's culture online, where job seekers can view actual photos of your employees building a house for Habitat for Humanity or read a short blurb about the latest project your firm completed and why it's important to the surrounding community, or view media articles where members of your firm are quoted or your projects have

---

[9] Source: McKinsey & Company, March 9, 2022 "Gone for now, or gone for good? How to play the new talent game and win back workers," By Aaron De Smet, Bonnie Dowling, Marino Mugayar-Baldocchi, and Bill Schaninger.

been featured. All of these things help tell the story that your company is an industry expert and that you have a firm culture that others want to be a part of. These are all meant to enhance what your company is doing and deserve to be shared beyond just your company's website.

Given all of these factors, I encourage my business-to-business (B2B) clients to build a company presence on LinkedIn® to maximize their digital branding efforts and serve as a critical extension to their company websites. I would encourage you, over the next few chapters, to think about your company's LinkedIn® page as the place where you post the latest news, cultural updates, and job-seeker information about your company on a timely and consistent basis.

Get on LinkedIn,® Section 5

Similar to Part I: Personal LinkedIn® Branding, Part II: Company LinkedIn® Branding also contains Calls To Action sections after each chapter. These exercises help you apply what you have read and encourage you to take action on the company LinkedIn® page based on your experience level as determined via the poll at the beginning of this book.

Novice = Let's build a company page together. (Scan the QR code for accompanying visuals for the step-by-step process.)

[NOTE: Although most of these functions can be performed via the LinkedIn® app, I recommend to my clients that they create the company page via the Desktop version of LinkedIn.®]

1. Sign in to your personal LinkedIn® account. [NOTE: You must a have a personal account in order to create a company page.]
2. At the top menu bar, go to "Work" and click on the down arrow. Then, scroll all the way to the bottom of that pull-up menu and click on "Create a Company Page."
3. Another menu will then appear, where you can choose to create a company page for the company you work for.
4. Once you click on "Company," a menu appears where you can create the company's page identity with a name, logo, tagline, industry, size, and other demographics.
5. Once you have created the company page, continue reading for more strategic tactics to implement.

Now that you have built the company page or have updated the existing company page to include more relevant demographic information, it's time to start posting. As a writer who suffers from writer's block by staring at a blank page with the full intention of writing, posting on LinkedIn® can stir up these same fears. One of the best ways to overcome this fear is to get organized and develop a social media editorial calendar. Akin to a magazine's editorial calendar, the social media calendar helps to map out the content to post each month, each week, each day, or even each hour throughout the day, if you are posting that frequently. The calendar should include the following, at a minimum:

- Dates and times of postings
- The topic to be discussed
- Written content for the post
- A visual element—a photo or, better yet, a video
- Link(s) for a Call To Action
- Author of the post
- Reviewer of the post
- Manager of the post to monitor comments, likes, and shares and to answer any questions that arise from the post
- Listing of various holidays, industry-specific awareness days/weeks/months, cultural days of remembrance, and company milestones to be recognized.

This social media editorial calendar will help track the various topics for the company page, create accountability for who is responsible for what on the company page, and help remind everyone of notable days of remembrance that the company can celebrate together. Scan

this QR Code to download a social media editorial calendar that contains design and construction themed holidays.

Experienced = Let's get analytical.

For those of you who already have a company LinkedIn® page that you are actively posting on, I encourage you to take a deeper dive into the "Analytics" page. From the company page in Admin view, click on "Analytics" to reveal the categories available:

- Visitors = Number of people that visit the company page
- Updates = Tracks the engagement of each post on the company page
- Followers = Number of followers on the company page, including some basic demographic information
- Competitors = You can self-select the companies on LinkedIn® that you consider your competitors and benchmark the number of followers, number of posts, and engagement "Impressions"

For my clients, I pull "Analytics" reports from LinkedIn® company pages once a month, to track the number of followers and to find out which post was most popular in terms of the number of people who saw the post ("Impressions"). I then break the reporting down further to determine how many people clicked on the link (the CTA) in the post. I compile these reports and share them with my clients each quarter to track their engagement levels on LinkedIn.® I typically meet with my clients to discuss which posts are performing really well and which ones are not and evaluate how the data will influence their digital content for the next quarter.

SET THE FOUNDATION FOR COMPANY ONLINE BRANDING

6

```
TALKS ABOUT:
#CompanyBranding #TrustedResource #ClientRecognition
```

With content marketing as the foundation for a company's digital branding strategy, LinkedIn® provides a strategic medium to guide potential clients and influencers of the company's brand through the sales funnel in the business-to-business (B2B) sector. I think we can all agree that posting on the company's LinkedIn® page should have an underlying purpose and strategy, with the end-goal to support sales. I am certainly not posturing that "x amount of LinkedIn® posts = x amount of sales," but strategic, quality, and consistent posting on the company's LinkedIn® page can support the company's B2B sales funnel to help guide potential clients from Awareness to Interest to Decision to Action.

There have been several debates in the sales and marketing industry that B2B sales funnels are no longer relevant in today's digital world. I would argue that the sales funnel is still applicable as a guiding practice, but will concede that the once-linear movement from Awareness to Interest to Decision to Action is no longer valid. The sales funnel movement now has many more twists and turns but still has the same end goal of influencing a potential buyer that *your* solution is the best one to help solve their particular business issue. Although there are several routes your potential clientele can take on their overall sales funnel journey, LinkedIn® company pages serve as a "free tool"—with no initial cost to set up the company page—to help influence your potential clientele. Although there are certainly costs associated with maintaining and growing the company LinkedIn® page, the overall branding benefits justify the costs when implemented strategically.

Types of Content to Post

When deciding what types of content you will post on the company LinkedIn® page, make sure your posts include at least three out of the four below characteristics:

1. Relatable
2. Authentic
3. Resourceful
4. Timely

LinkedIn® is a public, social network where almost anyone can view the company's posts. Make sure the content you are posting is relatable to at least your desired clientele by considering the following questions:

- What are some common issues that the company's clients are experiencing right now in the industry?
- What external factors are people facing in business right now that our company can help mitigate?

Although I completely advocate for sharing posts from other companies, I advise my clients to maintain a 60–40 ratio of posts they originate and posts they share from other sources. Posts that the company authors on their own help create a sense of authenticity and demonstrate that the company has a viewpoint and something relevant to share about a particular subject.

LinkedIn® company posts should also be resourceful. Meaning, they should help people in some way. Consider common industry problems or relevant feedback about a new statute that affects your clients. Creating resourceful content and sharing it out consistently will help build a following for the company page and build trust in the company's brand.

Timeliness should also be a key factor in the company's posts. If a new mandate takes effect next week, make sure you have posts either leading up to the deadline or on the day the mandate begins to demonstrate that the company is tracking important edicts that affect their business and the business of their clients. On the flip side of that notion, I also strongly advocate "throwback" posts to help capture a point in time in the past when the company achieved a significant milestone or to demonstrate just how far the company has come.

In addition to these posting characteristics, I have also outlined three types of LinkedIn® company posts that have been the most successful for my clients over the years. The company's social media calendar should include several kinds of these postings and variations on these themes as well, in addition to sharing posts from other LinkedIn® resources for a healthy digital mix of branded content.

Trusted Resource

When developing company LinkedIn® posts, consider the term I used in Part I: Personal LinkedIn® Branding: a trusted resource. This term applies to both your personal branding tactics, as well as the company's branding strategies. In order to become a trusted brand, you must first demonstrate that you can be a trusted resource and offer helpful information that your potential clientele may benefit from, just by following the company's LinkedIn® page.

In order to set that foundation of trust and credibility regarding the company on LinkedIn,® you need to show that the company has a pulse on the latest trends in the marketplace, that you are attuned to local news and media outlets that affect the industry, and that your company is involved in the surrounding community. All of these types of posts are not necessarily company updates, per se, but rather incorporate a myriad of outside sources, like media outlets and community organizations, that can help tell the company's story.

For example, any time one of my clients is quoted in the *Denver Business Journal* or by the local news outlets or in a design and construction trade magazine, I encourage them to create a post about it on LinkedIn.® Ideally, you would pull the quote from the article and attribute the author and publication, along with a headshot from whomever was credited with that particular quote and a link to the full article or news story video. This helps demonstrate that a third-party media outlet trusts the company enough to be included in whatever article is being published and that people at the company have noteworthy comments about a particular topic affecting the industry. That third-party recognition builds brand awareness for the company and needs to be shared on LinkedIn.®

Another example of a trusted resource post is when you share out relevant information in times of crisis that can be helpful to others, especially where your company does not directly benefit. For instance, during the last few days of 2021, the Marshall Fires devastated parts of Boulder County in Colorado. In response to this devastating disaster, one of my clients and

I devised an awareness campaign for donations to the Marshall Fire victims. These posts included graphics to encourage others to donate and informed others of the kinds of donations needed, from money to food to home goods, toys, school supplies, and everything in between. When you can demonstrate that the company cares and takes action during times of crisis where a true impact can be felt beyond just "thoughts and prayers," spreading the word via a professional network can reflect positively on the company.

Client Recognition

Another type of content to post on your company's LinkedIn® page is client recognition. These kinds of posts are when you use your own platform—the company LinkedIn® page—to recognize your client's achievements. When you post about what your clients are accomplishing, the benefits are two-fold. One is that you are paying attention to your clients, and two is that you are intrinsically tied to their successes.

For example, one of my clients is the American Council for Engineering Companies of Colorado (ACEC Colorado), and their main clientele are their members—consulting engineering and surveying firms. Any time we can highlight member firms on ACEC Colorado's LinkedIn® page—whether that's through video clips from a social media video campaign we put together about the best part of being an engineer, or celebrating an award that one of the member firms has won—we demonstrate that we are engaged with our clients and that we care about our clientele, where their successes become ours. When you are able to not only thank your clients for the past work you have done together, but also recognize your clients for their own achievements, you are laying the groundwork for a long-term business relationship, and not just a one-off transaction.

Company Expertise

This last bucket of content may seem obvious to some, but I still see several companies struggle with this, and that is to display your firm's expertise on the company's LinkedIn® page. Part of this challenge is to actually know what your company is an expert in—perhaps it is mass timber or affordable housing or sustainability practices, or perhaps you have certain key services that you offer in-house—instead of relying on an outside source for that expertise. Once that key area is identified, then you need to post about it consistently on LinkedIn® to drive home the message that your firm is, indeed, an expert on mass timber and why it's so critical to the design and construction process. Note that I am NOT recommending you post any trade secrets, but that you at least give clues as to what that trade secret is and leave people wanting to know more.

For example, a "Did You Know" or "#DYK" campaign is perfect to develop your firm's expertise on LinkedIn®—where you can post a series of content starting with, "Did you know that our firm has a whole sustainability division in-house that only focuses on LCA's (Life Cycle Assessments)?" and then proceed to tell people how and why this expertise will benefit your potential client.

If you are only adding this information to your website, you are missing out on a whole range of potential clients that could be receiving your message that your firm is the LCA expert. For instance, if you take the time to add a separate page to your website explaining your firm's LCA expertise, but then don't tell anyone about it (aka do not post about it on LinkedIn®), how are people going to know to visit your company's new website page? You must direct people to the new content you have created; you need to tell them what to do and guide them to your page in order to learn more about your firm's expertise. There's so much other noise that you are competing with in order to grab someone's attention online, so you need to direct them to your page by posting one or two pieces of relevant information as a "friendly reminder" that your firm just established this new sustainability department, or that your firm has been building this expertise for years and is finally sharing the breadth of your firm's knowledge and expertise with others in an attempt to set your firm apart from other design and construction firms in the industry.

LinkedIn® Analytics Overview

Now, let's explore these three kinds of content for the company LinkedIn® page through the lens of data. When potential clients engage with me to talk about their social media tactics, especially on LinkedIn,® the first thing I ask is, "What has been your most popular post thus far?" The typical response is a "deer in headlights" confused look accompanied by this verbal response, "Uhhh, what do you mean?" I then respond with, "Well, let me see your firm's past LinkedIn® analytics reports," which is then followed by a typical response of, "LinkedIn® has analytics?"

Any true marketing strategy needs some form of numerical data to help inform and direct you, as the marketer, as to what your LinkedIn® audience is responding to, where your LinkedIn® audience is based out of, and how often your LinkedIn® audience is engaging with your content.

These analytics are actually one of my favorite parts about social media, in that every single post is trackable. You can see when the post was created and who created the post (based on the Admins connected to and allowed to post to your company page). You can also track how many "Impressions" this one post received, e.g., how many people have seen this one post in their LinkedIn® feed. "Clicks" demonstrate how many people have actually clicked on the link in your post.

Another tracking type is the "CTR," which is a digital marketing term that equates to the click-through rate (the number of clicks that your post receives divided by the number of times your post is viewed by people on LinkedIn®), and you want this number to be high, as it demonstrates the overall engagement people have had with your post. (Scan the QR code for visual references to the examples below.)

Trusted Resource

During the height of quarantine, (April 1–May 31, 2020), ACEC Colorado wanted to demonstrate that the association was there for its members and was still serving its membership as a trusted resource with the latest information. If you recall during this time, rules and regulations were changing constantly for businesses, especially regarding the "essential worker" debate for design and construction professionals. ACEC Colorado still wanted to provide a means to connect directly with its members and to connect other member firms with each other. During quarantine, we found that the most popular posts were the original series of Digital Fireside Chats, where ACEC Colorado members could join a Zoom® call at a designated date/time to join in a discussion amongst their peers regarding a certain topic affecting the consulting engineering industry. This post demonstrated that members of ACEC Colorado were a viable resource with a voice and a message to share, and it resulted in an increased number of registrations for the next Digital Fireside Chat.

The second most popular post during this time was a post about funding resources for members. Again, at the height of quarantine, firms had many unanswered questions, like "Will we need to make layoffs?" and "Which projects are being put on hold, which are moving forward, and which are being canceled altogether?" We wanted to make sure that ACEC Colorado was a trusted resource for its members, so we made a point to share out any relevant business updates, such as alternative funding resources from the Colorado Office of Economic Development and International Trade, or the latest PPE (personal protection equipment) requirements on a construction site, or resources explaining the PPP (Paycheck Protection Program) loans from the Small Business Administration. During this time of crisis, when the risk of the unknown was prevalent, it was critical that ACEC Colorado reminded its members that they had a source of information they could trust and rely on to help their company remain open, retain its staff, and safely complete its design and construction work. At that time, so many different things in our businesses attempted to divert our attention, but if you visited and then followed the ACEC Colorado Page on LinkedIn,® you were receiving constant updates on the state of the industry, how to connect with people, and how to find alternative sources of funding during a crisis.

Client Recognition

As we discussed earlier, recognizing your clients and their accomplishments on your company's LinkedIn® page is mutually beneficial and lays the groundwork for a long-term business relationship. It shows that you are aware of what your clients are doing, outside of just the work you perform together, and it also demonstrates that when you use your company's page for content that is not solely focused on just your company, you are capable of sharing the spotlight and can use your platform to boost others.

Again, ACEC Colorado's clients are their members, and anytime we can highlight the great work that their members perform, it serves a mutually beneficial purpose. Each year, ACEC Colorado hosts the Engineering Excellence Awards and uses LinkedIn® as an outlet to share the award-winning project submissions. It is part of a campaign that recognizes each firm individually, where we create a specific graphic for each firm and tag each firm in an individual post, with a link to view all of the project videos. The post pictured on the supplemental online *Resources* page (scan this QR code to access) thanked and congratulated Muller Engineering Company for an Excellence Award and received 1,071 "Impressions," meaning over 1,000 people viewed this one post that highlighted a specific firm. This gave ACEC Colorado a platform where people could engage with Muller Engineering Company—to like the post, to share the post with others, to leave comments, or to congratulate them. I have to admit that these are some of my favorite posts to see on LinkedIn.®

To take this a step further, imagine that you see that one of your clients won a design award, or you notice that a partnering company recently had a project highlighted in a local media outlet. I would pay attention to these announcements and reshare them on the company LinkedIn® page, with content to the effect of, "Thanks so much for including our firm on this project, and congratulations on your ACE Award." It shows that you have relationships within the industry, that you partner with different firms, and more importantly, that you partner with award-winning firms. It's a much more subtle way to share information that is not perceived as "bragging." Your company proves that it has actual relationships with various companies and that your firm takes the time to recognize others and not always focus on just themselves.

Firm Expertise

As we reviewed earlier, this category of content is one of the most popular for company LinkedIn® pages, but you want to make sure you are highlighting your firm's expertise strategically. Let's take a look at some examples of how you can highlight what your company does best, but in a way that is engaging to your intended audience.

For example, ACEC Colorado posted a photo of Heidi Gordon, the association's executive director, and a link to a video where she was featured in a series of interviews for the Transportation & Construction Girl organization. This post demonstrates that groups outside of your firm value the people at your firm enough to interview them and highlight them for their expertise, and also that other organizations took the time to recognize an individual at your firm for a purpose. Although this particular post only received 430 "Impressions," the post generated 17 "Reactions"—where people not only saw the post, but then took the time to "Like" it or "Celebrate" it. Creating posts that generate a reaction from your audience is the basis for their overall engagement with your firm on LinkedIn.®

Another way to highlight your firm's expertise is to show your involvement with local municipalities and governing bodies. For example, for Engineer's Week, ACEC Colorado reached out to the governor's office for the State of Colorado and requested the official proclamation recognizing Engineer's Week in Colorado. This may seem like a standard task for the association, but if you do not tell anyone about it and do not post it on LinkedIn,® how will people know that your firm took the time to plan and reach out to local officials in order to recognize all of the good work that engineers do for the State of Colorado? This one post received 555 "Impressions" on a Sunday evening, the night before Engineer's Week started.

You always want to highlight what your firm does for others, whether it's your clients, your partners, or the local community. This demonstrates that your firm has established relationships and has a story to tell beyond just the company's projects and its employees.

Get on LinkedIn,® Section 6

Now that you have set the foundation for the company's online brand, it's time to get creative with the company's posts to become that trusted brand. Referencing back to PwC's company survey, which found that "top choices for drivers of trust among consumers were accountability, clear communications and admitting mistakes," let's explore a couple of examples based on your experience level.

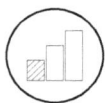

Novice = One way to build trust in the company is simply by posting the company's environmental, social, and governance (ESG) report each year. I encourage my clients to take the reporting a step further to provide analysis of the content as well, not just reporting the numbers. Provide context for the environmental benchmarks and what the company's plans are to improve them. Consistent reporting and admitting when the company does not hit its goals will set the foundation for trust in the company among clients and stakeholders.

Intermediate = Create a video campaign of common problems and solutions that your company solves for its clients. This can be done in an interview style by asking the corporate leadership team a few pointed questions regarding how the company helps others and what a few best practices for industry pain points are. This video campaign can be broken down into a series of one-minute videos that feature multiple executives answering the same question, such as:

> "What is the biggest missed opportunity right now in the industry?"
>
> "The biggest change I expect to see in the industry in the next 10 years is…"

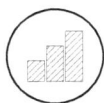

Experienced = To elevate that video campaign mentioned at the Intermediate level, consider interviewing your clients and featuring them on your LinkedIn® company page as part of a video testimonial series that demonstrates, from the source, how the company has helped others. Having a third-party endorsement from an actual client, explaining how your company helped them in a particular situation or during a difficult time, is another way to demonstrate transparency and trust.

TALKS ABOUT:
#PeopleDrivenCulture #Recruitment #Retainment

Whether we like it or not, change is inevitable, but it is often avoided, ignored, or approached with resistance, especially in corporate America. One of the most notable and recent changes to corporate culture arrived in the form of a worldwide pandemic that will arguably change company culture forever, regardless of your firm's industry, company size, or profit margin. In what business analysts are coining "The Great Resignation" or "Great Attrition," corporate America is experiencing a massive revolving door of employees. From people changing companies to ones that offer more flexibility to people leaving their current industry to work in a completely new one with little or no prior experience, to people exiting the workforce altogether with early retirements or instituting life-changes to be a full-time, at-home caretaker, all of this change affects your firm's culture and will reshape the way corporate America recruits and retains employees.

Instead of fighting against external factors and market conditions that we cannot control, what if we approached this upheaval of corporate culture as an opportunity for growth? Opportunities signify choices and strategies to be made, where you can set goals and milestones to be achieved over time. By shifting your firm's mindset about employee turnovers and changes and approaching it as an opportunity for growth, you can set the foundation to rebuild your firm's culture.

People-Driven Culture

At its core, company culture is driven by people—how we manage people, how we interact with people, and how we handle problems and implement solutions with people at our company. One of the ways to rebuild your firm's culture is to examine your company's core people and recruit others that will compliment this group, setting the foundation for your company culture. This exploration of who you are as a company and who you would like to recruit and retain to augment your firm's culture can be approached as an internal marketing strategy to hire and keep the best people.

This exploratory process can be initiated by answering the following questions:

- What are your firm's key values?
- How can you instill those key values into your recruitment process?
- What is your recruitment process to attract the next generation of your firm?
- What can your firm offer employees that other companies can't or won't in your particular industry or market segment?

- Once you hire these new employees, what is your firm's retainment process?
- How is your firm paving the way for employees to grow and excel at your company?

This internal review process of your company's culture and how you can rebuild it sets the foundation for how you portray your firm externally. Consider the old adage, "Build it, and they will come." One way to rebuild and share your firm's culture is to show people who you are as a firm on LinkedIn.®

Example:

I am currently working with Concepts in Millwork, a 40-year-old millwork company in Colorado that has recently faced several employee changes that will leave a lasting impact on the firm's culture. This family-owned business has grown exponentially from 10 employees in 1982 to nearly 100 in 2022, and is now working on multi-million dollar construction projects. In line with most construction-related firms, this company is also constantly recruiting for the next generation of employees to replace the retiring Baby Boomers and overcome the stigma of the construction trades to demonstrate lucrative career paths in construction without college debt.

One tactic we are currently implementing resulted from the corporate leadership's internal review meeting that took place in December 2021 to reevaluate employee processes and initiatives. During this meeting, the core group devised a list of words that they wanted their company to embody moving forward. An excerpt of the list of adjectives included:

- Compassion
- Unity
- Celebration

- Gratitude
- Family

This list of key values is now being used as part of their social media strategy on LinkedIn.® We are building a social media campaign that focuses on each word to share its meaning and significance to the company and how the firm is embodying this word with its people. One example is a recent "unity" post that I wrote the content for and created a photo collage to demonstrate how this firm is inclusive, engaged, and working together to achieve the same goal.

u·ni·ty (noun) [as defined by Dictionary.com]

- *a whole or totality as combining all its parts into one.*
- *oneness of mind, feeling, etc., as among a number of persons; concord, harmony, or agreement.*

Over the past 40+ years at Concepts in Millwork, we have worked tirelessly to unite not only all the parts and pieces of construction projects for our clients, but also to unite all of our people—our employees, families, and friends. Despite the challenges over the past few years, Concepts will continue to unite to overcome things that seek to divide us. This unity of coming together as a family-owned company with a common purpose allows us to better serve our clients and our people.

Tomorrow is never promised, and there is no time like the present to come together and combine all of our parts and pieces into one.

#ConceptsInMillwork #Unity #MillworkCompany

Go to https://www.linkedin.com/feed/update/urn:li:activity:6914229395792551936 for the actual LinkedIn® post and accompanying photo montage. (You can also scan the QR code for the online *Resources* page.)

Without ever meeting anyone from this company or stepping foot into this millwork plant, one can glean, just from this LinkedIn® post, that this is a family-owned company and that they are focused on working together. As the social media campaign develops and is shared consistently online via LinkedIn,® the firm is setting the foundation to rebuild its company culture around its key values, which can be used as a recruitment tool to attract others who want to be a part of these key values.

Employee Recruitment

Once you have identified your firm's culture and how you want to rebuild it for company growth, explore ways in which you can incorporate your firm's culture into your employee recruitment process. Consider, for a moment, the potential new employees' perspectives and how they are approaching the job-seeking process.

When people are considering a job change or career change, it is not so much that they are chasing a job title, job description, or even a higher salary (we all know money is important, but not everything). It is more that people want to make sure they will be a good fit with that new company, hence why company culture is so important. Even though you can state your company values and mission on Indeed.com, how can you actually demonstrate your company culture and values online in an authentic way?

One answer lies in creating that culture on your company's LinkedIn® page. Post the fundraiser your firm is sponsoring for the local children's hospital to gather funds for the new wing. Post about those catered lunches that your company offers twice a week. Post about your company's involvement in industry associations and how employees are encouraged to donate their time to learn more and network with industry professionals. All of these posts start to form the narrative of your firm's culture in a digital setting.

Construction Focus: Employee Recruitment

Workforce development has long since been a challenge for the design and construction industry, even before the "Great Resignation" was coined. From Baby Boomers retiring in higher numbers to a decreased number of people entering the construction trades to an overall cultural belief that construction is not the industry of choice to pursue, employee recruitment has become even more challenging. The typical outlets of in-person career fairs and visits to local high schools and trade schools have been limited or non-existent over the past few years. So, without the opportunity to shake hands, meet the next generation of your workforce, and share stories about what it is like to work at your company, how are you conveying your firm's culture to potential new employees?

One way to capture your firm's culture and actually control the message of what it is like to work at your firm is to strategically post on your company's LinkedIn® page. Post about your firm's mentor-mentee program to show that your company is invested in its employees. Post about the training funds available for employees to use after they celebrate their one-year anniversary. Post about employee success stories, such as workers who may have started at your firm as interns and have now been brought on full time. All of these posts help frame the backdrop of your firm's culture and what your company does to make sure they are hiring and keeping the best people.

Employee Retainment

Now that you have used LinkedIn® to create that captivating story of your firm's culture, how are you now retaining your current employees? We discussed earlier how you can highlight your firm's expertise with your principals or company owners being quoted in local publications or perhaps speaking at a local conference, but your principals are not the only ones at your firm with expertise worth sharing.

Your project engineers and cost-estimators, your project architects and designers, your engineers-in-training, your marketing specialists, your business development team—they are all doing things in the industry that are worth sharing. When a member of your team earns a certain certification, a simple "Congratulations!" goes a long way. Or when a project manager takes their own team to volunteer on Saturdays for two months at Habitat for Humanity, highlighting their volunteer work shows the heart of your employees. These are all great ways to recognize the efforts of your employees online and retain them as well.

These activities demonstrate that your firm's employees take initiative, that they care about other people besides themselves, and that they are actually willing to spend time with their coworkers outside of work. By posting these activities on your company's LinkedIn® page, you can set the foundation to rebuild your company's culture and help you recruit and retain top talent at your firm.

The Need for Online Company Culture

Regardless of the pandemic and any future situations affecting our workforce, we can no longer ignore the need to establish an online company culture. This digital age allows for people in different cities, states, and even countries to all work for the same company and, hopefully, embody the same company values. How are you connecting all of those people without flying everyone down to the Bahamas for a corporate retreat? Make use of a professional social platform, like LinkedIn,® to connect your employees online.

In addition, hybrid workplaces are on the rise and are most likely here to stay to accommodate a more diverse workforce and offer the flexibility most employees are seeking. With varying people working in the office on different days, how are you making connections with and then staying connected to your employees and colleagues? Online company culture can be demonstrated and experienced via LinkedIn® to share those celebratory moments and recognize your employees' expertise.

Regardless of your employees' physical location, you can still share more about what your company is doing as a whole. Use your company's LinkedIn® page as a news source for your employees to learn more about what other departments are doing to advance company culture. You can share out new company initiatives, groundbreakings on new construction projects, and company milestones.

Another consideration is how to onboard new employees without a robust Human Resources (HR) staff that is easily accessible. With changing corporate policies of at-home vs. on-the-job training, HR has been forced to become more creative in how they address employees' needs and help drive company culture. Consider making LinkedIn® part of your onboarding process to ensure that new employees have updated their current company listing on LinkedIn,® to check that they are now following your company's LinkedIn® page, and to have them connect with other employees on LinkedIn® to help build an online network of connections.

How to Rebuild Your Firm's Culture on LinkedIn®

Now that you have firmly established your company's culture with its key values, understand the need for an online company culture, and have a general idea of the various ways you can demonstrate your company culture online, we can now take a deeper dive into more of the specifics of strategic online posting on your company's LinkedIn® page.

Whenever I begin working with a new client to manage their company's LinkedIn® page, one of my first questions is, "What do your employees do together that isn't actual work?" I often receive immediate objections to even sharing this information with me, much less an external social platform. Other typical responses include "Why do you want to know?" or "Why does that matter?"

My response to those questions includes the notion that most people know what kind of work a construction company performs and can name at least a few projects that company has completed. But how do you answer the question, "What is your company culture like?" The best response to that question SHOULD be, "Take a look at our company's LinkedIn® page."

One of my favorite examples of capturing firm culture is from ACEC Colorado's virtual holiday party. The reason I included this example is to show the CTR in the Analytics section, which LinkedIn® defines as "Clicks/Impressions." This one post shows smiling faces, over the top holiday costumes, and tons of ugly sweaters, and it has a 66.5 percent CTR. (Scan the QR code for a visual reference to this post.)

Now, the post only received 165 "Impressions," but of those 165 people, 110 of them clicked on the update to read more—nearly two thirds of the people that actually saw this post in their LinkedIn® feed clicked on the link to view more.

The photos I posted capture the fun we had that evening and make people want to be a part of that. Have some fun with your firm's culture postings. People like seeing photos of other people because it's engaging, and it really encourages others to be a part of your firm.

Get on LinkedIn,® Section 7

Now that you have started to rebuild your company's culture via LinkedIn,® let's sign on to your company's LinkedIn® page and take action to share your people-driven culture online.

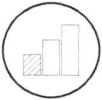

Novice = Highlight what your company does for its employees outside of work. This can include:

- Company lunches and celebratory get-togethers
- Happy hours (check your company's policy on drinking and posting pictures of employees with drinks in their hands)
- Support for those who are going back to school or undergoing training
- Volunteer efforts as a firm
- Post an article recently published about a project your firm recently completed or where a member of your firm is quoted in an online story
- Share a photo and online link about a personal award that one of your employees received or a firm-wide recognition your company was bestowed for a recent project
- Recognize certain "days" or "weeks" of the year that relate to your company:
  For example, in the A/E/C industry, we recognize Women in Construction Week in March or National Professional Engineers Day on August 3. I created this Social Media Calendar for the A/E/C industry. (You can also scan the QR code for the *Resources* page to access this document.)

(NOTE: I do not recommend posting for every single day of recognition available, only those that relate to your industry, your company, and/or your employees.)

Intermediate = Share your firm's expertise online without giving away your company's "secret sauce."

Create a series of posts that contains best practices for common problems your clients face and how your firm is best equipped to solve them. This kind of post can also be used on company proposals to demonstrate your firm's differentiators.

Designate an employee or social media consultant to provide "live" event coverage for an employee that is attending or, better yet, speaking at an industry conference. Share real-time quotes and updates from that event.

Create a themed "thank you" campaign to say thank you to your employees for their hard work in order to achieve a company goal or recent changes you have made as a firm. Extend that themed "thank you" campaign to your clients and thank them for the opportunity to work together to complete this notable project and for helping your company grow.

Experienced = Use a social media calendar like this one I created for the A/E/C industry. (You can also scan the QR code for the *Resources* page to access this document.)

Here are some ideas for inclusion:

- Share out one-minute video clips from interviews with top executives to share:

- Why did they choose this industry?
- What is the one piece of advice you have for new-comers to this career path?

- Create personalized social media campaigns that tie into industry-themed occasions, like Women in Construction, National Safety Week, etc., that include photos of your employees, video clips as to the importance of that themed occasion, and live coverage from an event your company hosted for that occasion.
- At the end of your company's fiscal year, compile a themed social media campaign that encapsulates all of the milestones your firm achieved in that year. You can do this to both highlight your internal employees and company achievements and recognize what you did for your clients in the past year.

LEVERAGE THE COMPANY'S ONLINE BUSINESS DEVELOPMENT STRATEGY

8

> **TALKS ABOUT:**
> #CompanyBranding #BusinessDevelopment
> #OngoingRelationships

Throughout this book, we have learned that business development (BD) is building long-term, mutually beneficial, professional relationships based on problem solving for each other. The oxygen mask metaphor states that before you can help others, you must first help yourself to know who you are, what you believe in, and what your overall vision is for yourself, so that they become the building blocks of your personal brand. We have also learned that in order to build out your BD network and leverage your personal brand, you must find connection points with others and consistently share helpful, timely information with your network to keep people engaged.

These same notions and tactics can also be applied to a company's BD strategy. Now that we have explored several ways to capture and share the company's online brand, as well as ways to rebuild company culture through strategic online messaging, it's time to take action and leverage the company's online brand to support its overall BD strategy.

In the presentation I gave to the National Association of Women in Construction's Business Development Industry Council, entitled "Tips and Tricks to Business Development: Create Value for Your Clients and Capitalize on the Trust You Have Built with Them to Win More Work," I identified several BD practices that can activate or reactivate companies' BD strategies. Below are a few of these tactics that can be applied to your company's online BD strategy to create value for your clients, build trust, and help the company win more work.

- Research market trends and industry leaders
- Find creative ways to connect
- Create ongoing relationships

Research Market Trends and Industry Leaders

Conducting market research about trends and industry leaders within the company's sector creates a knowledge base for the company's online BD strategy. When I am helping my clients build their BD strategy, I typically pose the following questions:

- What are some common pain points affecting the industry?
- What external factors are affecting the marketplace?
- What solutions to these pain points and external factors can your firm offer that others can't?

Answers to these questions can be found by using the "Search" function on LinkedIn® to do market and competitor research. LinkedIn's® "Search" function has grown exponentially to include not only searching for individual people, but also for services, companies, jobs, postings, industry groups, courses, schools, and even events.

As an example, I typed "construction Colorado" into the "Search" function, and a number of groups came up that I could now request to join or "Follow" to learn more about industry trends. Based on that one search item, I am now plugged into several construction groups, such as the Colorado Construction Professionals, Colorado Construction & Design Industry Pros, and others. These groups allow construction professionals to post helpful industry information, event registration notices, and best practices. This is also the forum where you can ask about common pain points and external factors affecting the marketplace. Join these groups to be an active member, asking questions, responding to others' requests, and sharing resources in order to set you and your company apart from others as part of the company's BD strategy. (Scan the QR code to access the visual for this "Search" function.)

LinkedIn's® "Search" function can also be used to conduct competitor research to help your firm answer these pivotal questions:

- Which firms are winning the projects your company wants?
- What can you offer that those firms can't or won't?

To initiate this research, I typed in "construction Colorado" with the "Companies" filter turned on, which resulted in a number of construction firms in Colorado that I used as part of my competitor research. I advise my clients to follow as many company pages that are relevant to their industry as possible, so these company posts and updates will now automatically show up in their LinkedIn® news feed. With this information at your fingertips every time you open the LinkedIn® app, you can keep a pulse on what projects your competitors are completing, what jobs they are hiring for, what industry events they are exhibiting at, and who from their executive team is consistently being quoted in the media. The best part about this competitor research is that you are not having to look up individual company websites. All of this information is housed in one place, on LinkedIn,® and can serve as a valuable tool as part of your market trends and industry leader research.

For example, my "construction Colorado" company search resulted in a number of firms that I could access to learn about all of the latest news regarding these firms. For instance, by clicking on one of the company pages listed, I noticed that Flatiron Construction created a series of video posts called "Flatiron in Focus," which highlights various employees' journeys on their construction careers. These short, one-minute videos are a great recruitment tool to demonstrate how people, especially young people, are making their way into the construction industry. This is a strategic marketing campaign that makes use of videos, which are the most engaging type of content on social media, enhancing the company's brand and encouraging online engagement.

Another type of market research you can conduct on LinkedIn® is industry news. Again, without visiting each of your competitor's websites where up-to-date information may or may not be posted, LinkedIn® is a convenient source where the latest industry news is posted almost every day. Using LinkedIn's® "Search" function, you can self-select what kind of news and updates you would like to see in your feed by typing in "construction" or "marketing" or "engineering" or "social media"—to name a few. You can also choose to be subscribed to an organization's newsletter that they push out over LinkedIn.® I encourage my clients to follow a variety of industry news sources for a well-rounded view of what is taking place in their industry and which companies are included in these updates.

As mentioned earlier, the "Search" function can also be used to look up individual people on LinkedIn.® For company BD purposes, I encourage my clients to use this "Search" function whenever they are interviewing for a particular project to learn more about the interview team. In design and construction, most projects are awarded based on a formal proposal and an interview process where companies submit their written proposals by a certain due date for review. From there, a short-list is created based on the company's qualifications and written narrative about why that certain company should be selected for the project. The short-listed firms are then invited to do a presentation or "interview" for the construction project.

Once shortlisted, I encourage my clients to find out who is on the selection committee and then conduct "people research" on LinkedIn® to learn more about the people they need to convince to award their team the project. Scouring personal profiles of the interview team members can help you identify connection points between them and your company's team members. For instance, did anyone from your company's interview team attend the same university as one of the selection team members, have you worked at similar jobs, what organizations do they belong to, and what are their interests outside of work? Arming your company's team with as much information about the audience they will present to helps direct the messaging, tone, and tactics used during the interview process. This information can help your company set itself apart during the interview process by establishing rapport more quickly with the decision makers—helping your company win the job they are interviewing for.

Find Creative Ways to Connect

Online company business development on LinkedIn® is based on a series of connection points between the company and its online followers. In order to bolster the number of followers on the company page, companies need to find creative ways to connect and tell an impactful story online. Below are some of the typical LinkedIn® updates that I initially recommend for my clients.

- Project updates: Celebrating the completion of a project, sharing lessons learned from a project, or recognizing when the project wins an award
- People updates: Sharing media articles that company leaders are quoted in, celebrating those that have completed training courses or licensures, or highlighting company employees that are presenting at conferences
- Industry updates: Posting quarterly industry market indicators based on internal data points and/or external industry research, sharing out the latest economic development reports from the company's local markets, or updating monthly labor reports for workforce development

In addition to these content ideas, there are several other ways companies can engage with followers on LinkedIn.® These include creating a poll, sharing event registrations, and self-publishing articles and newsletters. (Scan the QR code for the visuals to accompany this section.)

- Create a Poll: LinkedIn® allows you to poll your audience and learn more about them directly through your company page. As one of the post types at the top of your company page, once you click on "Poll," a menu pops up where you can ask pointed questions from your followers, such as, "What is most important to you when working at a construction firm?" You can even ask what kind of content they want to see more of on the company page.

- Create an event: To encourage more registrations to your company's training events or to cross promote another organization's event that your company employees are attending, you can add an event to the company page. This is another way to demonstrate what your company offers to its employees and to create more visibility around the topics and issues the company cares about via its employees' participation in industry conferences and events.
- Self-published articles and newsletters: LinkedIn® has expanded its content marketing options to allow companies to post articles directly on LinkedIn,® instead of just including a snippet and a link to an article that may be hosted on another site. You can also post company newsletters to LinkedIn.® (NOTE: I advise my clients not to post any confidential or internal-only company information on LinkedIn.® Be intentional and strategic with public-facing information.)

Create Ongoing Relationships

In order to create ongoing relationships via the company page on LinkedIn,® you need to first understand what the company's most popular types of posts are, who is engaging with the company page, and how they are engaging with the company page. The best way to gather this information is via LinkedIn® "Analytics" on the company page.

I recommend that my clients track and document the company page analytics each month and analyze it in quarters. So, looking back at Q1, how many followers did you gain? How many followers did you lose? Which post had the highest number of "Impressions" over the past quarter? What kind of content do your followers prefer—photos, article links, videos, polls, etc.?

Once you start building your database of analytics over the years, you can begin to notice trends in the time of year or even time of day that you post. The analytics I keep for my clients document those incremental increases over the years for upward trends in the number of followers and rates of "Impressions," but remember, this took years to develop. It takes time, a lot of content, and consistent engagement with followers and comments to reach these levels.

It is important to note that I am only addressing ORGANIC content. Paid social media advertising and boosted posts are a whole other book that I will most likely never write, because short-term paid advertising strategies are completely different than long-term branding strategies. Yes, it does take longer in terms of time, but for B2B service-based companies, in my experience, I have found that organic content engenders more trust about a company and helps drive home the fact that you do not need to pay for followers or pay for "Impressions." LinkedIn® is still a FREE platform, but it takes time to develop that brand, gain followers, and increase the number of "Impressions" on your content.

Some of the top questions I receive when speaking with a potential LinkedIn® social media client are, "How many followers is good?" or "What can we do to increase our followers?" My answer is to not obsess over followers. Yes, the number of followers does influence the number of people you are reaching who are consistently viewing your posts, but do not live and die by the number of followers on your company page. Followers will come, as long as you are putting out quality content that your audience finds engaging on a consistent basis. I always recommend to my clients that if you are going to obsess over a data point, focus on the number of "Impressions" you are receiving for each post. This will help guide what you post, when you post, and how often to post to help drive up those "Impression" numbers. As your number of "Impressions" starts to increase and more people share your content, the number of followers will also start to increase because others see the value of your content and don't want to miss out on it.

Track Your Analytics

As referenced previously in the book—where we reviewed several examples of posts, looking at how many people saw the post, clicked on the link in the post, and shared the post—those are all analytics that you can track and monitor on your company page. (Scan the QR code for more visuals and examples.) Make sure you set a reminder for yourself each month, as the social media manager, to capture your company page's analytics. I recommend tracking the following two metrics:

1. Followers: Track how many you have gained each month
2. Updates: Track which posts were the most "popular" by gauging the number of "Impressions," click through rate, etc.

As a caveat to that, I would caution to, again, follow your company's branding policy and not just continue to post whatever has the most "Likes" on your LinkedIn® page. However, you can use that information to guide you.

For example, video content has statistically shown to be the most popular type of content on social media. Short, one-minute "get me to care" videos catch people's attention and can do wonders for your company's branding and social media impact. However, you do not need to make every post a video post. Create a substantial mix of content with photos and links and save your most important messaging for video content, since it is shown to be the most popular type of content on social media.

Once you have a deeper understanding of the types of content that are receiving the most traction on the company page based on the LinkedIn® "Analytics," you will then need to start posting more often in order to create and maintain these ongoing relationships with the company page followers. (NOTE: Each industry and company type will eventually develop its own "rhythm" to posting, whether that is every day, as in seven days a week, or five days a week to mimic the typical work week, or three times a day, or even just once a week. The frequency of LinkedIn® postings will also vary depending on the time of year and what your company has going on. For instance, your company policy may be to post during the work week, five times a week, with informational posts and some celebratory or project milestone posts.)

What about when one of your top executives is speaking at an upcoming national convention and you really want to drive people to attend their presentation and perhaps even gather some questions/issues from LinkedIn® members that your top executives can answer? To create online engagement, you can create a poll on your company page, then take the most popular requests to develop a social media campaign addressing these topics. You can also create a video series with your executives addressing the top, burning questions on a certain issue. Then you can post photos of your executives as they are listed in the conference's program with a link to register for the conference or sign up for your executive team's presentation. During the presentation, you can have a designated social media contact to "report" on the presentation—taking photos of the audience and capturing live, one-minute video clips of important points/conclusions that your executive team made during the presentation. After, you can share out a "thank you" post from your executives to everyone that attended and perhaps include a link for more information about a certain topic.

Whatever the frequency of your company's postings, it can always be increased. The more content you gather and create, the better off you will be when it comes time to decide what to post. I like to say, "If it didn't happen on social media, did it REALLY happen?" Think about posting on social media as a means to document what is going on at your firm, so by the end of the year, you can look back at your company's LinkedIn® page and have an accurate and timely history of what your firm accomplished over the past year. You can then share that out as an end of the year review in December or as a look back over the previous year in January.

As always, be intentional, strategic, and professional with your postings, especially the posts on the company page. Increasing the frequency of posting just for the sake of posting is not always effective. If you post too often, you could lose followers, or people may miss an important piece of content because you are posting so often—it gets lost in the fold. Again, your company page is a way to control the branding and messaging about the company and how your firm is being perceived online.

Leveraging the company's online BD strategy via LinkedIn® is an essential component to the company's overall BD strategy. It can offer supplemental market research information, provide creative ways to connect with others who can advocate for the company online, and create ongoing relationships with people who support the company and who can help become online brand ambassadors for the company.

Get on LinkedIn,® Section 8

Let's explore a few ways to leverage the company's online business development by getting on LinkedIn.®

Novice = We have firmly established that in order to be a trusted resource, you need to help others. In fact, the Sophisticated Marketers' Guide to LinkedIn® recommends that you "spend 80 percent of the time HELPING others and 20 percent of the time trying to solve your own problems" in order to be viewed as authentic. (Scan the QR code for a visual reference.)

One way to do that through the company page is to actively answer people's questions and calls for help on LinkedIn.® I encourage my clients to interact with others through the company's page by simply scrolling through people's posts on LinkedIn® to find questions that your company can answer. For instance, perhaps someone posts a question like, "What are some best practices for writing case studies?" If your company writes case studies in the B2B sector, like I do, I would respond back to that individual under my Business Rewritten profile and share a couple of tips, along with links to some of my favorite case studies.

By simply responding to others' questions online, the company can demonstrate its expertise and show that they are willing to help others, all of which builds trust in the company's brand.

Intermediate = Create your own "News Source" and/or "Company feed" for your employees and clientele on the company page. (Scan the QR code for a visual reference.)

Most of us are so distracted all day—between our personal and professional lives—that often times, we don't even know what's happening at our own companies and/or one department has no idea what another department is doing. Several companies are also still adjusting to hybrid work environments where people are not in the office every day at the same time. To keep everyone informed, create a newsletter on LinkedIn.®

From the company page, click on "Write Article" and the following page will appear, where you can post a company article. To take it a step further and create a company newsletter, click on "Create a Newsletter" to have the next menu pop up where you can build out the newsletter theme and content, then publish it on LinkedIn.®

Experienced = **Create a leads group that the company hosts and invite other companies to partner with you to share best practices and industry leads.**

When you sign into LinkedIn® (NOTE: I recommend doing this from your laptop, as opposed to your smartphone), look up at the top right next to your personal profile. Then follow the next steps to create a leads group.

1. Click the down arrow on the "Work" tab, then click on "Groups." This will bring up the groups you are currently a part of.
2. Then click on "Create Group."
3. From there, you can set your group rules and establish your group name.
4. For my leads group and others that are for members only, I recommend keeping the group "Unlisted," so when others on LinkedIn® use the "Search" function,

unless they are a member of the group, the leads group will not appear in the search items (NOTE: I choose to keep this closed off because it builds trust within our group that the information we share is only accessible to our group.)

5. You can then "Invite Connections" to join your group.
6. As the Admin of the group, you can monitor who can join the group, what people in your group are posting, and several other functions to help you manage the group effectively.

I found that this leads group format on LinkedIn® really helped hold people accountable. It goes back to that old adage, "If you don't post it on social media, did it really happen?" In order to stay in the leads group, each person needed to post at least one new lead per month. Whether that was a new proposal bid for an upcoming project or perhaps information from a recent event or conference where there was new information shared out from a development panel, each person in the group needed to contribute some bit of information to share with the group. Again, if you didn't post in the group at least once a month with a viable lead, I removed you from the leads group. This helped hold people accountable and ensured the group was full of people who wanted to share information, so that we could all benefit from the group's collective knowledge. It took a while for people to adjust to this system, but the ones who stayed in the group benefited the most, and we were able to develop lasting business development relationships.

When quarantine hit and we could no longer meet once a month in person, where we reviewed the postings on LinkedIn,® we shifted our leads group entirely to LinkedIn,® where we were all posting more frequently about resources that would help all of our businesses—from information about PPP Loans to which projects had been put on hold and which construction sites were still open. We ended up creating this body of knowledge that was online and accessible to everyone in the group. And as I'm sure you know, certain mandates and regulations were changing constantly at the time, so it was valuable to have an online resource where we could all post the latest developments and updates for our industry in one single location. LinkedIn® provides a great way to conduct virtual business development to have a platform to share your knowledge with others, but in a very concerted way that shows first-hand that you can provide value to a team and/or group.

Q: **Is there a better time of the week or day to post, when click-through rates and impressions are higher?**

A: *Let's flip back to earlier in Part II, Company LinkedIn® Branding, where we reviewed the "Best Times to Post for Your Business" for LinkedIn,® and this rule of thumb mimics what most Public Relations experts would tell you: The best days to post are typically Tuesdays, Wednesdays, and Thursdays.*

Also think about your clientele's habits—and this may vary by the type of person you are trying to reach. If you are a B2B company that is trying to get in front of top executives, consider their work-week.

Sunday evenings, they are probably checking emails and prepping for the week, so that could be a good time to post since there are no other distractions.

Mondays are bad because they are typically filled with meetings and phone calls from the previous week or back to back video conferencing calls.

Tuesday through Thursday, they have a bit more flexibility, and you can catch them browsing LinkedIn® in between meetings and project work.

Friday afternoons are typically a bad time to post because people are checked out or hammering through a deadline to wrap up before the weekend.

In terms of the time of day, if you are just starting out and are looking for a bit more engagement and more "Impressions," then stick to the early morning hours and late afternoons (between 5:00 p.m.–6:00 p.m.).

Q: I know a person that seems to post every three hours, and I asked him if he ever got any work done. He replied that he has a service that posts for him. What do you think about that?

A: *I would consider that posting service as an ad hoc consultant who is managing that person's social media. Now, if that person is posting every three hours on their feed, that is quite a bit of content to share out so frequently, but maybe that person has a personal goal to increase his follower count or number of connection opportunities.*

I would caution that some people may be turned off by that frequency of posting. Instead of gaining followers, as that person may have originally intended, he may actually be losing followers, because if I see someone coming up in my LinkedIn® feed every three hours with content, I might think that they are spamming me.

When you hire an outside service or social media consultant to manage either your own personal social media or to manage your company page on LinkedIn,® there must be a baseline of trust between the consultant and whomever that consultant is "representing" online. Think of it as essentially giving someone else the keys to your brand and letting them drive.

I would strongly recommend against a "bot service" and actually have another human being manage your social media. I would also recommend getting to know that person and asking them the tough questions, like "How would you respond if there is a negative or damaging comment left on a post?" or "Do you have a strategy in place for follow ups when someone leaves a comment saying, 'We should connect,' 'Let's get together soon,' or just 'I owe you an email?'"

I would also recommend reviewing your company's social media guidelines with that consultant. Review hardline Do's and Don'ts and rules you have to follow concerning OSHA guidelines for safety in your photos on construction job sites to more detailed conversations about "What is your firm culture?" or "How would you like your company to be portrayed online?" These are all important conversations to have before someone else takes over your company's brand online. Just be selective and make sure that outside service is on brand for your company.

Q: Do you have any suggestions on how to get more views on our company's LinkedIn® posts? Should we have our engineers reshare what the company is posting to reach a broader audience?

A: *The short answer is YES! Yes, yes, yes, yes! So, step one would be to make sure that all the engineers at your firm have a LinkedIn® profile, showing a current headshot (within at least the last two years) and their most current place of employment (your company) and demonstrating that the engineers are actually following your company page. I can't tell you how many companies have hired me for their LinkedIn® strategy where the leadership team and half of their engineers aren't even following the company page that they work for!*

BEST PRACTICE TIP: Make LinkedIn® part of your company's onboarding process. Review that person's LinkedIn® profile together and make sure that person has indicated that they work at your firm and that they have the right title. I have actually seen where people give themselves promotions on LinkedIn® and have "boosted" their title to manager—when that person is clearly NOT a manager.

So, to get back to your original question, yes, one of the best ways to increase the number of "Impressions" for your company page and increase the rate of engagement—and this is also low-hanging fruit you can take advantage of—is to have all of your employees follow your company's LinkedIn® page. Then take whatever you post on your company's LinkedIn® page and have each of the engineers share that out with their own personal network, which thereby increases the number of people that can see your company's LinkedIn® posts.

I like to describe this effect as dropping a pebble in a pond, which creates a series of ripples. The post on your company's page is the pebble being dropped in the pond, and the ripple effect that will increase the number of "Impressions" for that post is carried out by your engineers that are now sharing out that one post to each of their own personal networks.

This is also a "safe" approach to increasing your number of "Impressions" without your engineers going "rogue." For instance, you do not want your engineers posting about a company project that may be getting put on hold or perhaps has been cancelled. The safest bet is to encourage your employees to share what is posted on the company page because, hopefully, you have already put processes and procedures in place to have the content on the company page reviewed and approved before sharing.

ASSESSMENT: LET'S TAKE A POLL, AGAIN

Remember those poll questions you answered at the very beginning of this book?

Take the time to reassess and find out if you were able to move up from Novice to Intermediate or Intermediate to Experienced or Experienced to Expert status on both your personal and company branding on LinkedIn.®

1. **How often are you on LinkedIn?**®
   a. *My LinkedIn® is tied to an old business email that I can't access anymore*
   b. *Once a month*
   c. *Once a week*
   d. *Every day*
   e. *Multiple times a day*

2. **What are you currently using LinkedIn® for?**
   a. *To find a new job*
   b. *To find out where people I know are working*
   c. *To make strategic connections*

d. To post on my company's LinkedIn® page

e. To manage both my personal and company LinkedIn® profiles

3. **What is currently on your LinkedIn® profile?**

a. An old(er) headshot and the last company I worked for

b. Current headshot, current company name and title, and my current job description

c. All of b., plus an introductory paragraph in the "About" section, and associations I participate in

d. All of c., plus "Skills" and "Recommendations" sections endorsed by others

e. All of d., plus a personalized tagline, personally branded "About" section, and "Volunteer" and "Interests" sections completed

4. **How are you managing your company's LinkedIn® profile?**

a. I didn't know my company had a LinkedIn® page

b. I know my company has a LinkedIn® page

c. I follow my company's LinkedIn® page and click "Like" on some of the posts

d. I am regularly sharing my company's LinkedIn® posts and sending content to our marketing team to post on LinkedIn®

e. I manage my company's LinkedIn® page and set quarterly strategies and goals based on LinkedIn® "Analytics"

If you answered mostly A's and B's = Novice LinkedIn® Level
If you answered mostly C's = Intermediate LinkedIn® Level
If you answered mostly D's and E's = Experienced LinkedIn® Level
If you answered ALL E's = Expert LinkedIn® Level

Now, it's time to share your LinkedIn® progress! Find the screenshot you took at the beginning, before you made any changes to your personal and/or company LinkedIn® profile, and prepare your Before and After post.

Take a screenshot of your new and improved profile. Then post on LinkedIn® and tag me @Julie M. Wanzer, LEED AP, including the hashtag #LinkedInBeforeAfter.

Scan the QR code to view one of my #LinkedInBeforeAfter moments that I recently made.

CLOSING

Thank you for participating in this deep dive on LinkedIn.®
My hope for each of you is that you have learned at least
one tip, tidbit, or best practice that will help elevate your personal business development strategy or that of the company you
work for.

Despite the current environment and external factors that
may or may not be affecting our ability to connect in person, we
all need to be able to connect digitally. Business is already moving in the direction of project teams forming with people that
live all across the nation, whom you may never have the chance
to meet in person, so you need to find connection points with
people and be willing to be that trusted resource to help yourself
and others succeed in your chosen careers.

HIRE ME TO SPEAK

Julie Wanzer, LEED AP, has provided professional speaking engagements on several marketing and business development topics, especially in the architecture/engineering/construction industry for eight years, since becoming the owner of Business Rewritten, Inc.—a marketing consulting firm that tells stories in the built environment. She is based in Denver, Colorado, serves clients nationwide, and loves to travel for speaking engagements.

Wanzer is also an active member of Innovation Women, an online "visibility bureau" helping drive visibility for entrepreneurial, technical, and innovative women through speaking engagements.

Email julie@increasingmarketvalue.com to inquire about a specific topic for your internal team or for an upcoming conference, or visit businessrewritten.com.

View Business Rewritten's YouTube channel to check out examples of Julie Wanzer's presentations.

Learn more about who has hired Wanzer for professional speaking services:

- American Council of Engineering Companies of Colorado
- Associated General Contractors of Colorado
- Colorado Contractors Association
- Society for Marketing Professional Services—Southwest Regional Conference

BUSINESS *Re* WRITTEN

Business Rewritten (BR) is a marketing communication firm, founded in 2015 and based in Denver, Colorado, that tells stories in the built environment. Julie Wanzer, LEED AP, is the Owner and Principal of Business Rewritten and describes what drives her by writing:

> *"My purpose is to help my clients discover, write, and share the real story behind every building façade."*

These stories, in both the vertical and horizontal built environment, come in all shapes and sizes and can be told through various mediums—from digital and social media content to one-minute "get me to care" videos and social media campaigns, to researched and impactful case studies and published articles.

We produce the best outcomes for our clients at the intersection of transparency, strong communication, and personalized connections, with a specialty in the design and construction industry. Learn more at businessrewritten.com.

BR Services

1. Award Submittals: To gain recognition for your projects and your people
2. Digital Content: To inform clientele of your personal differentiators, as well as the company's expertise via case studies and blogs
3. Social Media Strategy: To create engagement with you and your company's social media channels
4. Video Storytelling: To get people to care about your projects, your company, and your people through impactful visuals and interview content

The B Corp Movement

Dear reader,

Thank you for reading this book and joining the Publish Your Purpose community! You are joining a special group of people who aim to make the world a better place.

What's Publish Your Purpose About?

Our mission is to elevate the voices often excluded from traditional publishing. We intentionally seek out authors and storytellers with diverse backgrounds, life experiences, and unique perspectives to publish books that will make an impact in the world.

Certified

(B)

Corporation

Beyond our books, we are focused on tangible, action-based change. As a woman- and LGBTQ+-owned company, we are committed to reducing inequality, lowering levels of poverty, creating a healthier environment, building stronger communities, and creating high-quality jobs with dignity and purpose.

As a Certified B Corporation, we use business as a force for good. We join a community of mission-driven companies building a more equitable, inclusive, and sustainable global economy. B Corporations must meet high standards of transparency, social and environmental performance, and accountability as determined by the nonprofit B Lab. The certification process is rigorous and ongoing (with a recertification requirement every three years).

How Do We Do This?

We intentionally partner with socially and economically disadvantaged businesses that meet our sustainability goals. We embrace and encourage our authors and employee's differences in race, age, color, disability, ethnicity, family or marital status, gender identity or expression, language, national origin, physical and mental ability, political affiliation, religion, sexual orientation, socio-economic status, veteran status, and other characteristics that make them unique.

Community is at the heart of everything we do—from our writing and publishing programs to contributing to social enterprise nonprofits like reSET (https://www.resetco.org/) and our work in founding B Local Connecticut.

We are endlessly grateful to our authors, readers, and local community for being the driving force behind the equitable and sustainable world we are building together.

To connect with us online, or publish with us,
visit us at www.publishyourpurpose.com.

Elevating Your Voice,

Jenn T Grace

Jenn T. Grace
Founder, Publish Your Purpose

www.ingramcontent.com/pod-product-compliance
Lightning Source LLC
Chambersburg PA
CBHW040859210326
41597CB00029B/4902